A Minnesota Mom

In the land of the Ancient Mother

VOLUME III

The Making of a Missionary

PATRICIA CARLSON STENDAL

Unless otherwise noted, Scripture quotations are from the KJV

Addresses are in back pages of book

Library of Congress Cataloging in Publication Data

Stendal, Patricia C. 1930-

A Minnesota Mom in the Land of the Ancient Mother
Volume III: The Making of a Missionary

1. Minnesota – 1960's. 2. Mexico 1960's – Married life. 3. North Dakota – 1960's. 4. Missionary Training. 5. Wycliffe Bible Translators. 6. SIL Summer Institute of Linguistics. 7. JAARS. 8. Gifts of the Spirit – Hearing God's voice – MAF Missionary Aviation Fellowship. 9. Lives of influential missionaries – Jungle Camp. 10. Missionary Call – Tzeltal Indians. 11. Answers to children's prayers – Survival Training. 12. God's provision.

Artwork by Osvaldo Lara
Layout by Martha Jaramillo R.

ISBN 978-1-62245-038-1

Printed in USA
By LIFE SENTENCE Publishing
www.lifesentencepublishing.com
Like us on Facebook

Dedication

To my dear friends:

Majel Meyer
Eugenia Dean
Ruth Haase
Elvira Mikkelson
Bernice Haase
and the others of
the Tuesday morning
prayer meetings.

These dear women, almost all of whom are now a part of the cloud of witnesses who have joined the church triumphant, are now looking down from their special places in the great arena of the heavens. (Heb. 12:1)

They prayed me to the point of victory so that I could respond to the missionary call.
They prayed me through SIL.
They sewed all the special gear that was required for Jungle Camp.
They prayed me through 2nd year SIL and the first years in Colombia.

They pooled their meager resources to buy me the special things I needed for my missionary outfit – perma-press sheets, etc. and Oswald Chambers book, My Utmost for His Highest.

Majel was in a class by herself as she set up a cattle program to help with our support.

I pray that through the Lord's strength, I have lived up to their expectations.

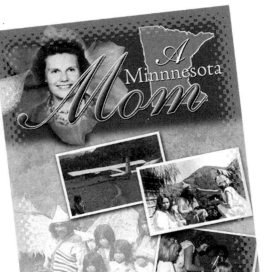

A Minnnesota Mom

In the Land of
the Ancient Mother

VOLUME I
Beginnings

PATRICIA CARLSON STENDAL

A Minnesota Mom

In the Land of
the Ancient Mother

VOLUME II
A Vision is Formed

PATRICIA CARLSON STENDAL

Synopsis

This is Volume 3 of a proposed six volume series. Volume 2 of this series, *A Vision is Formed,* was the story of a very timid little girl who by God's supernatural dealings in her life eventually became a pioneer missionary in the mountains of Colombia. Volume 1, *The Beginnings,* gives an overview of the missionary work of the Stendal family, some of the spiritual history of the Stendal/Carlson ancestors, and a short biography of two Indians who risked their lives to invite the Stendal family to live with them on the outskirts of this very reclusive and closed tribe.

After many dealings of God in their lives in their home state of Minnesota, Volume 2 closes with the arrival of Chad and Pat Stendal with their three children at the University of North Dakota to begin their training to be members of the Wycliffe Bible Translators, a mission dedicated to bringing the New Testament to all the unreached language groups of the world. After a tremendous spiritual struggle, Pat finally agreed to rent their home in a suburb of Minneapolis. This was not only a struggle for Pat, but all four of the grandparents were very much opposed to this venture. Chad was a successful civil engineer, and Pat had a degree in Elementary Education and had taught in the Minneapolis Public Schools before becoming a full-time mother and home maker. Even their pastor counseled that their spiritual gifts and training could be better used in Bloomington, MN, than risking their lives and those of their children in a foreign country with a primitive group of tribal people.

Chad had been eager to answer the call to missions some three years previously, but Pat was not ready at that time. Six-year-old Russell was strongly in favor of this project. His prayers had played a large part in moving the family forward. He had even contributed $15 from his small savings account to pay his mother's registration fee to attend this summer linguistics course at the University of North Dakota.

Family finances were tight, but God had supplied the money needed for tuition, board and room, and child care at the university. Their church where they had labored intensively in volunteer children and youth ministries gave them a party and a going-away gift of $50, which was just the right amount to rent a trailer to haul all their summer equipment, including bicycles, children's toys, games, and books, to their destination.

Introduction

In the time of the '50's and '60's after World War II, a great missionary emphasis among Christians in the United States arose. Christian groups had been active among the servicemen during the war. A renewal of Christian faith and interest in the Bible took place among the men and women involved in serving their country. Although for some their renewal might be called "foxhole conversions," many stuck and resulted in changed lives. Service men had been overseas, especially in the South Pacific, and they came home burdened for the native people they had seen whose lives had been disrupted by the war.

Groups such as Intervarsity and Campus Crusade ministered to students on the university campuses. Youth for Christ and other para-church organizations were active among high school and college young people. Missionary organizations in England and the USA had already sounded the call for the gospel to be carried to the last people group and language on earth. Resounding slogans, such as, "Why should anyone hear the gospel twice until everyone has heard it once?" made an impact on the Christian population. World Vision to help the orphans left by the war and the Wycliffe Bible Translators to bring the written New Testament to every people group in their own language were just two of the missionary groups formed or that gained new vitality. The missionary departments of denominational churches and Bible Institutes also shone with new vibrancy. Recruits and money were needed. Churches formed groups, such as Go ye! Pray ye! Give ye! Based upon Bible verses in the King James Bible, young people were encouraged to go, older people to pray or give. It was felt by many that when the last tribe of people was reached with the gospel, Jesus Christ would set in motion the end-time scenario as stated in the book of Revelation and other Scripture portions. Missionary groups, such as New Tribes, proclaimed that everyone should be on the foreign mission field unless God had especially called one to stay in the home country. It is against this backdrop that the following true account takes place.

Image Credit to Townsend Archives

Table of Contents

Volume III
The Making of a Missionary

Volume III

The Making of a Missionary

"My grace is sufficient for thee; for my
strength is made perfect in weakness."

Jesus Christ
2 Corinthians 12:9

Acknowledgements

I want to thank Jim and Jan Walton
for letting me use their pictures of SIL,
Jungle Camp, and the first year in Colombia.
I also want to thank my daughter, Gloria,
for all her time in locating all the pictures and
placing them in their proper place within the text.
A blank page is anathema to Gloria.
Thanks too to all of you who read the manuscript
over the years, proofed it, and offered suggestions,
particularly Jeremiah Zeiset
at Life Sentence Publishing and his staff.

Chapter 1

Stage One

Grand Forks, North Dakota
    Summer, 1962

"Well, I guess we certainly know beyond the shadow of a doubt that this is where God wants us," remarked Chad as the small gray Mercury with the U-Haul trailer behind pulled up in front of an ancient structure, labeled temporarily SUMMER INSTITUTE OF LINGUISTICS on the University of North Dakota campus. A strong tail wind had blown against the large rear expanse of the trailer and helped our tired old Mercury arrive.

Studious-looking young people were ambling along grassy paths and across the paved parking lot, notebooks and textbooks in their arms. The girls looked trim and fresh in summery dresses, and the men looked efficient in their colorful short-sleeved shirts and informal trousers. They all seemed young and organized.

It was early afternoon on a cool, moist June day in North Dakota. I was still in emotional turmoil from the aftermath of the packing, the sad farewells of the grandparents, and the cheerful send-off from the church. Compared with these sharp-looking young people, I felt dull, drab, old, and laden with family responsibilities. Russell, prone to carsickness, had been vomiting, and the odor permeated the vehicle.

Chad left us in the car and went into the building. I waited in the car with the children to find out what the next step would be. We were here. That was all I knew. We waited and waited. It seemed that Chad would never return. The children were getting restless and tired of being cooped up in the car. Russell turned white, opened the car door, and started vomiting into the street by the side of the curb. Sharon took one look and promptly threw up all over herself, me, and the front seat of the car. "Go find your father quickly," I shouted at Little Chad, and then he too was gone, glad to be out into the fresh air.

Two girls in pastel cotton dresses crossed the street in front of the car. They gave me friendly smiles as they went by. I recognized them as students from Bethany Missionary Training School near our home in Bloomington, Minnesota. "Oh, Lord," I prayed, "I have made a terrible mistake. I should never have come here with all these children. What am I going to do now?"

We waited and waited. Russell lay down in the back seat and shut his eyes. I knew he felt miserable. Sharon fussed in the front. She wanted a drink; she wanted to get out of the car. I vainly mopped at my dress with a greasy rag I found under the front seat.

All of a sudden, Chaddy was at the car window. "Daddy wants you to come in. You have to take a test. We children are supposed to wait in the car."

Adrenalin flowed into my system. This was going way too far. The audacity of them to even think of giving me a test before they had shown us where we were to sleep. If this was the way they treated missionary volunteers, I was ready to quit right now. I was ready to tell them just what I thought of them.

Into the building I strode. Chad was standing with a group of people about our ages or a little older, smiling and talking. These were clearly some of the staff members. They didn't seem to notice my soiled dress or my ill humor. After greeting me briefly, a woman led me into the next room. She was in charge of the phonetics department, and she immediately gave me an oral phonetics test to determine my background in phonetics and my native ability in mimicry. I was placed in the lowest group.

In due time, we were taken to our dormitory building where three rooms in a row had been reserved for us. Each one contained two single cots, two desks, two chairs, and two chests of drawers. Linens and army blankets were provided by the University. We soon unpacked, set up some semblance of organization, and were ready to start classes the next morning.

The lectures that first morning were dreadful. The instructors must have been up all night planning their unintelligible presentations. Nothing made sense to us at all. As we left one lecture, Chad turned to a short, dark-haired young woman walking beside him and remarked, "Was that Greek to you too?"

"No," she responded, with just a touch of a foreign accent, "To me it was Chinese." Later we discovered that she was a native of Greece, and Greek was her first language. After engaging in conversation with fellow students during the lunch hour, we discovered that only those who had some previous linguistic study really understood what was going on. The instructors were going over our heads.

In addition to a hearing problem, I was now having trouble with my sight. An eye specialist had remarked after examining me a few months before, "Half of your sight is in your eyes and the other half is in your brain—there's nothing wrong with your eyes." Where did that leave me?

Genie Dean, one of the ladies in the prayer group, suggested that I go out to Bethany and have the pastors lay hands on me for healing. She set up the appointment, and I was anointed with oil and prayed for. One of the pastors assured me that I would be all right, however this first week at SIL my eyes bothered me terribly.

Chad and I were both graduates of the University of Minnesota. His degree was in Civil Engineering, and mine was in Elementary Education and Social Studies. Neither of our backgrounds had prepared us for these courses in linguistics. In addition to all our other assignments, those of us who wanted graduate credit had to write reports on extra assigned reading in linguistic journals. We were cautioned to not let this work fall behind as towards the end of the summer our other assignments would be so heavy that we would not have time to do the graduate requirement. I went to the library and checked out the journals, but try as I would I could not read this fine print. Everything directly in front of my field of vision would blur when I looked at it straight on. Besides, the vocabulary was unfamiliar, and I didn't understand the concepts. Praying without ceasing, I plowed into the journals. By the time I had the children settled for the night, it was almost time for the library to close, so I didn't have much study time. Suddenly, I discovered that by sort of looking out of the corners of my eyes, and not really focusing on the page, I could make out the words. Using my skim reading skills, I scanned the articles and wrote up the reports as best I could. I received a passing grade on them all, and after about two weeks, I realized that my eyes were back to normal again.

As a child I had greatly enjoyed the lazy summer afternoons when Mother took us to the lake for swimming or picnics. I hated to think that my children would be cooped up in a hot nursery all these beautiful summer days while we studied linguistics. To my surprise, I found that the school-aged children, including Russell, were being taken to the university pool three times a week for Red Cross swimming instruction. Every afternoon, recreational swimming was available for those who cared to participate. The children greatly enjoyed the day-care program and learned to love those who were in charge, many of whom were the teen-aged offspring of our linguistics instructors. We all became like one big family, and the children delighted in their new acquaintances. Recreational evenings were a weekly part of the program, as well as special prayer times and daily chapel services. As I got to know them better socially, I couldn't figure out how such lovely Christian people as our instructors were outside of the classroom could be so completely unintelligible in class.

Our first quiz came in phonemics class. (Phonemics is the science of forming an alphabet once you have the phonetic sounds written down.) I had no idea at that time what we were even supposed to be doing, but I managed to pull a "C." Russell knew that we had been given a test and asked to see my paper. To my horror, he began to upbraid me soundly. "I have paid my money to send you to school here," he scolded, "And I don't want it to be wasted. You have to do better than this." I realized that this was exactly what Chad had told him when he came home from the Christian Day School with "Cs." He had ended the year with a straight "A" report card. Could I be expected to do as well?

Gently I explained to Russell that I was going to need his help to get through this course at all. He agreed to help with the care of the younger children so that I would have more study time. Each morning we met together for a family devotional time. We communicated our problems honestly with the children, and they held us up in prayer. Soon we were oriented enough in the basics of linguistics to ask intelligent questions. We were over the hump.

I was happy to renew acquaintance with Vurnell Newgard. I had known her as a child in Sunday school and again as a teenager at Pioneer Girls' camp. Now she was Vurnell Jacobson, and together with her husband, Elwood, was enrolled in one of the advanced classes. Their area of interest was Viet Nam. Elwood had already been serving in that country for several years, and they were now third year students. It was good to see someone out of my past in this strange new place.

I had not realized beforehand how hard it would be for me to adjust to eating in a group situation. The children and Chad seemed to get along all right, but I just couldn't seem to feel satisfied. Nothing tasted quite right. A number of common foods had never been served in my childhood home because of the preferences of my parents. Unthinkingly I had avoided these items in my own menus unless Chad had especially requested the dish. Now I was faced daily with foods I had always avoided. Also, I was unaccustomed to being limited to three meals a day. I had always before in my life had free access to a kitchen where I could snack and nibble as I liked. This situation focused in on the fact that food was of great importance in my life, and that part of my reluctance to go to a foreign country had been the knowledge that I would have to change my comfortable accustomed eating habits. This move to the University of North Dakota campus was the first step to leaving my familiar comfort zone. I actually shed tears over Mother's homemade sugar cookies that I munched between classes. After they were gone, I found that a mid-morning coffee break with a sweet roll or doughnut and an ice cream bar in the afternoon helped to fill the psychological void. (Remember, I come from a long line of plump Swedish ancestors used to morning and afternoon coffee.)

Each student was required to devote one hour of time each day to a work assignment. I was on the vegetable crew along with the young Greek couple, several other students, and a fascinating young man who had grown up in Africa, the son of missionary parents. As we chatted around the huge basin of potatoes or carrots to be peeled, John entertained us with tales of growing up in Africa. Here was the end result of the life we were all choosing for our children. He assured us that the mission field was a terrific place for children to grow up. I confessed to him my fears that the lure of the world would suck away my boys in their teen-age years. "Don't worry about that," he responded, "By that time they will know that there is something better in life."

John was familiar with several foreign languages and seemed to be on an inside track when it came to linguistics. Several times he was able to help me when I got lost in the fast pace of the grammar classes. I was almost sorry when the staff decided to relieve the mothers of small children of the daily work assignment, feeling that we had enough extra work already.

The worst class of the entire course for me was the phonetics class. We had to reproduce vocally every sound that could possibly be made by the human mouth, nose, and throat. We also had to learn to recognize every sound in the International Phonetic Alphabet by sound and symbol. We would need this skill in order to write down the previously unwritten language once we got into the tribe. Our future tribal language could contain any combination of the 300 sounds in the International Phonetic Alphabet. There was no way to predict which ones we would need to know, so we had to learn them all. My hearing was not too sharp, and in general I had about zero native ability in this area. Every Friday we would climb to the top floor of a large brick building, enter a small room, stand in front of an instructor who was sitting behind a desk, and reproduce all the sounds that we had been taught that week. I was probably the most hopeless student they had that year, but all my phonetics instructors were supportive and encouraging. They didn't want me to drop the course just because of my inability in phonetics. Several encouraged me with the idea that the Lord probably had a tribe just waiting for me with a language only containing the sounds that I could say. However I had an ongoing dialogue with the Lord in which I was constantly telling Him that there would certainly be no point in my going to a foreign country if I couldn't even make the sounds required for this phonetics course.

Every Friday afternoon as I walked to the building and climbed the stairs to the third floor, I would be talking to the Lord, first in English, then as I came up the stairway, I would switch into my "prayer language" which by this time had progressed a bit beyond the ka-ga-ba stage. I would then open the door, go into the little room, and I was able to say all the sounds to the teacher seated behind the desk. She would then put a mark after my name on her list. Friday after Friday, the same miracle would take place. At last, at the end of the course, we had to say them all. (As I remember, it was all, or at least a good representative list.) And I did it! I was not able to say those sounds correctly before or after, but in that little room, I was able to do it every time!

University
of
North Dakota

Summer Institue of Linguistics
Box 8217, University Station
Grand Forks, North Dakota
Summer of 1962

Chapter 2

Accepted?

As we attended the Wycliffe orientation meetings, we became more and more assured that we should apply for membership in the Wycliffe Bible Translators, so we made an appointment for an interview with the candidate office. After reviewing our background and missionary call, the assistant secretary advised us to apply as linguists if our grades at the end of the summer session were high enough. "We can get pilots and teachers," he said. "The bottleneck is translators."

Together with the children, we laid the matter before the Lord in prayer. From that point on, our grades took a turn for the better.

After several more interviews, we were told that at the end of the summer, we would be interviewed again and evaluated by the actual candidate secretary who would be coming up to North Dakota from Norman, Oklahoma. Then, subject to his recommendation and our final grades, the board would act, and we would be accepted or rejected. Physical examinations for each member of our family would also be necessary, and Chad and I would each have to take a test on basic Bible knowledge.

I had suffered most of my life with strange muscle aches and pains, and most recently my left shoulder and neck had been bothering me, but the examining doctor did not seem concerned about it, and we all passed the physical with flying colors.

Near the end of the summer I was called into the candidate office for an interview with the candidate secretary who had at last arrived.   After reviewing his assistant's notes, the secretary started asking me questions about my childhood and wrote my answers out in longhand on sheets of white typing paper. Each answer led to more questions, and sheet after sheet of paper was filled with writing.   Time passed. Meanwhile, Chad was impatiently waiting outside with the children, wondering what could possibly be taking so long. At last he could stand it no longer. In he came. He soon realized that the problem in the secretary's mind was my father. The more I described him, his work with the Gospel car, and his doctrinal position, the more concerned he became. He was afraid I might be a high pressure, arm-twisting, evangelizer, an attitude that would not go well in some of the delicate situations in which Wycliffe worked, especially Colombia, the country we had listed as our only choice. Finally Chad broke in. "We have highest respect for Patty's father, but we don't necessarily agree with him."   The secretary was satisfied and gathered up all the papers which are probably still on file somewhere in the candidate office.

Our final grades were all boiled down to two at the end. We both got "As" in grammar and "Bs" in phonology. Even Russell was satisfied. We were also accepted as junior members of the Wycliffe Bible Translators and the Summer Institute of Linguistics. The next step would be Jungle Camp in southern Mexico in January.

Back in Bloomington, we found our house spotlessly clean and in perfect condition. Mother and Dorothe had placed food in the refrigerator. The renter's wife had been a compulsive housecleaner, it seemed. The neighbors said that she sent the children outside everyday and spent her time cleaning the house. Even the rafters in the basement had been vacuumed. The Oriental rug that Chad's parents had been so worried about was still on the floor. It had been shampooed and had never looked more beautiful. Later, when we had gone to Colombia, Chad's mother reclaimed it for the floor of her new home out at the lake.

Chapter 3

Guam

Just before we left Grand Forks, we were called to a meeting of all the newly accepted members of the mission. The financial policy of the Wycliffe Bible Translators was that each one of us was to trust the Lord for our financial support. We were to give full information to churches and individuals upon request, but we were never, never to ask for money. "Full information without solicitation" was the motto. The mission would send a letter to our church explaining that we had been accepted by the Wycliffe Bible Translators and would be involved in deputation activities (speaking in churches, and making our plans known) for the next few months until we went to Jungle Camp in southern Mexico in January. It was expected that our church would ask us to speak and that they would assume responsibility for at least a good share of our support.

I had been corresponding with Majel Meyer over the summer. Majel and her husband, George, had been short term missionaries in Peru. Seeing the need, they had prayed for 1,000 new missionaries for the Amazon Basin. Shortly after their prayer, five missionary men had been killed by a tribe of primitive Indians in Ecuador. This event was world-wide news and focused much attention on foreign missions. Majel felt that this publicity would result in 1,000 new missionaries, but when these volunteers were not forthcoming, Majel wrote a book entitled *Where Are the Thousand?* This book played a part in my call to missions. I saw myself as a person who had been called, but who didn't go.

On the way back to Minnesota, we decided to visit both my relatives in South Dakota and also Majel Meyer and her husband who had a large ranch not far away. I had explained in my letters that her book had played an important part in my spiritual preparation for the mission field, and she had invited us to stay a few days with them. Majel turned out to be a capable, friendly woman of middle age. She radiated competence and energy. She and her husband, George, who was much more reserved, were starting a program to raise cattle for missions. Majel and George were thrilled with my testimony and the fact that we were already on our way to South America. They showed us their herd of Black Angus cattle, and suggested that we try to start a herd of our own. While it wouldn't help us for a while, the calves would provide a good share of our financial support in years to come. The Meyers would administer this program for us and furnish the pasture. We were thrilled with the idea. Here was a way to provide our own support. We decided to liquidate all our personal assets, including our Spartan house trailer, and purchase mother cows. Thus encouraged, we returned to Minneapolis where Chad went back to work for the U.S. Corps of Engineers, and we enrolled both Russell and Chaddy in the Christian School.

It turned out that the church going-away party had been just that. Many people thought that we had already gone to Colombia when we left for Grand Forks and were surprised to see us back. We had been involved in so many of the church activities that quite a few people had to undertake added responsibilities when we left. As one friend put it, "After you left, we found out that you and Chad had been running the church, and we didn't even know it." The church had recently changed pastors, and they were intent on plans to build a new sanctuary which indeed was badly needed. The church leadership was not interested in taking on more missionary support. No one asked us about our financial needs, and we told no one.

At one point the new pastor came to visit us. He explained that going to the mission field was fine for young people right out of Bible College, but that for an established family like us with small children to strike out on a missionary venture was sheer folly. I thought of our friends from SIL who were being welcomed back to churches and families that were behind them in their call and were happy to send them out. Outside of Majel and George Meyer, no one seemed happy about our plans. Chad asked for a meeting with our church board, laid our call before them, and asked their opinion. No one raised a doubt as to the authenticity of our call. Several stated that as we had been such faithful energetic workers in the church, we would probably do great on the mission field. After this meeting, one couple came to visit us and promised to send us five dollars a month when we went to Colombia.

I now realized another reason for my reluctance to go to the mission field. My family took great pride in their refusal to accept offerings. Although my dad, Dick Carlson, admitted that there existed a Scriptural basis for a full-time ministry, his model was the Apostle Paul whose tent making had sustained him and his companions. To him this was a nobler position, and he would consider it to be a personal disgrace should any of his family accept offering money.

On Chad's side of the family, we had Russell and Jean Stendal who had bravely struggled through the depression years, refusing to accept relief (now known as welfare). A part of the basis for their rejection of churches and organized religion was the opinion that the church was just out to get people's money. These two ideas had been so drilled into my head that I just could not stand any association with phrases such as "raise support." The only basis on which I could go to the mission field was trusting completely in God to supply our financial needs.

Part Three: The Making of a Missionary

My spiritual food and fellowship was now coming from the ladies' prayer group and the infrequent occasions when we attended Bethany. I felt that we needed a strong group of prayer warriors behind us when we went to Colombia. I started agitating to change churches. However Chad was reluctant to make a change after being a part of this church for ten years. One Saturday while in a supermarket doing the family shopping, I felt especially sad about our lonely situation. In our daily chapel services at the University of North Dakota, we had enthusiastically sung many all-but-lost hymns that our director Dr. Richard Pittman had resurrected out of history for us. Many of them had greatly touched my heart and blessed my soul. I wandered sadly down the rows of canned goods, thinking about the fact that the letter from Wycliffe had asked our church to conduct a commissioning service for us. I knew that they would probably not do it. A line from one of the hymns we had sung that summer came to mind, *Mine the mighty ordination of the pierced hand.* The thought lifted my spirit. The Lord Himself was sending us out!

Chad finally agreed to put a sign before the Lord concerning changing our church membership. It was definitely answered, and we resigned from the church and applied for membership at Bethany. We made it clear to the elders at Bethany that we were not asking for financial support, but only prayer support. Chad was surprised by the warm welcome that awaited us at Bethany. A number of our old friends greeted us with open arms. Chad was invited to speak at the Men's Fellowship.

We composed a letter telling of God's dealings with us thus far. We asked for prayer support, but only implied by quoting two lines from a hymn that we were financially dependent on the Lord's provision: *When we reach the end of our hoarded resources, The Father's own giving has only begun.*

Our "hoarded resources" were holding out. We were making plans to sell the house, furniture, and other personal items. Chad was back at his job with the Corps of Engineers.

We were saving money to go to Jungle Camp. According to the mission policy that had been explained to us, a quota was set up for each country. This meant the money that was considered to be necessary to support one adult for one month, according to the economy of the country. Children were figured at a percentage of the adult quota according to their age. In order to enter into financial relationship with the mission and leave for Jungle Camp, we would need (in addition to basic equipment) three months' support for our family per the Mexico quota and a signed statement that we were debt free. This would need to be accomplished by the first of January.

In late October, Chad came home from work one evening tremendously excited. Another job opportunity had come to his desk. This time the position was to be in charge of all the construction on the island of Guam, and he had all the qualifications. The opportunity was for two years, the salary was large, and the entire family could travel to Guam together. Chad had been in Guam in 1945 and loved the place. His thinking went this way: We would still go to Colombia eventually, but first we would spend two years in Guam, relaxing on beautiful white sandy beaches, no mosquitoes, and no malaria. There was even an indigenous tribe on the island whose language I (Pat) could analyze in my spare time, (so his thinking went). If they lacked a New Testament in their language, I could do that too. We would give at least a tithe of our income to the Colombian branch of the Wycliffe Bible Translators. In fact, the young, struggling branch might prefer the money to our physical presence.

This proposal fell on my spirit like a dash of ice water. I find it hard to shift gears anyway, and now that I was headed for Colombia via Mexico, I didn't want to get side tracked, but Chad brushed off my objections and continued with his enthusiastic plan.

At the supper table he continued in the same vein, expounding the therapeutic effect of the climate of Guam on our health. I timidly suggested that there was nothing wrong with our health, but he brushed that aside, going on and on about the beautiful beaches. At last six-year-old Russell could stand it no longer. He spoke up in the firmest, deepest voice he could muster, "I thought God called us to be missionaries in Colombia."

"He did, son," replied Chad, "And we are still going to do that, but first we are going to this beautiful place."

Once again Russell's firm, deep voice interrupted, "Do we have to take the easy way?"

The words of the child pierced Chad to the heart. He fell silent for a long time. The lovely vision of the island of Guam faded from his mind. Finally he spoke, "You've got a point there, son. We'll have to be very careful about this. Maybe it's not such a good idea." By the time we went to bed, he had decided against Guam, but the next morning, there was the enticing notice on his desk again. He picked up the phone and dialed our home number; the trip to Guam was on again.

The next morning, I felt extremely ill. The following day, a neighbor took me to the doctor, and an X-ray revealed that I had pneumonia. I called Chad at work with the news. "Oh, no!" he gasped, "not pneumonia!" He instantly remembered the time in 1958 when he had stepped out of the Lord's will and was struck down by pneumonia on the fourth of July. He instantly gave up Guam, and I made a speedy recovery.

In late November, a typhoon struck Guam. All American families were sent back to the United States, and the arduous reconstruction of the island began. If he had gone to Guam, Chad would have had to work long hours and receive no pay for overtime because of his rank, and we would have had to maintain two households: one on Guam, and one in the States. We would not have made a lot of money and the children and I would have been separated from Chad for a long time. By this time we had already set our course for Jungle Camp and Colombia, but this news confirmed to Chad that he had made the right decision in turning down the Guam opportunity.

Chapter 4

Renewed Faith

Burnsville, Minnesota
Nov. 1962 - Jan. 1963

Our house was not selling. We decided to rent it with an option to buy. A renter was found. Some of our furniture would have to be sold, but basically it would be rented furnished. As the plan was taking shape, I felt an icy fear start clutching at my heart. It had been such a relief to have this house in which to raise our children. How could I give it up? As I was thus meditating, the Lord spoke to my heart: *And every one that hath forsaken houses, or brethren, or sisters, or father, or mother, or wife, or children, or lands, for my name's sake, shall receive an hundredfold, and shall inherit everlasting life.* (Matt. 19:29)

In a few hours the mailman came. We were now on the mailing list for the Wycliffe Colombian Branch, and their newsletter was in the mailbox. As I opened the envelope, one item caught my eye. A large building with six apartments had been rented in Bogotá to house the missionaries who were already starting to arrive. The first house of the promised hundredfold had already been provided.

Part Three: The Making of a Missionary

The celebration of Christmas had caused a problem in our family almost as far back as I could remember. As a young child I had memorized *The Night Before Christmas,* and my mother knew *Annie and Willie's Prayer,* a very sentimental poem something on the order of *Dickens' Christmas Carol,* which she had recited once in a school presentation. However sometime in my early childhood, things started to change. My father's spiritual mentors did not approve of the celebration of Christmas. To them it was a pagan festival that had no part in the life of a Christian. Dad was fond of quoting Galatians 4:10-11. *Ye observe days, and months, and times, and years. I am afraid of you, lest I have bestowed upon you labour in vain.* He brought home a tract, which influenced Mother quite a bit. It was called, "My Lord Hath Not Told Me to Do It." It made the point that nowhere in the Bible were we commanded to celebrate Jesus' birth. In fact we were not even told the date on which it took place.

I don't know how this teaching affected the homes of Dad's associates, but it certainly caused havoc in ours each December. Each year, around December a major family argument occurred. Dad felt obligated to enforce a strict non-observance of the season, while Lois, a family friend who often lived with us, was determined that we children have a merry Christmas. Mother was halfway in between, and Grandma maintained that the arguing was ridiculous.

As far as Santa Claus was concerned, we had always been told the truth by our parents, but Dorothe and Darrell enjoyed the make-believe of the custom. Jolly red-faced men with white whiskers were one of my many phobias, so I stayed far away from all such. Lois generally succeeded in filling the house with Christmas cheer and our long stockings with gifts, while Dad held himself as aloof as possible.

After Lois' departure for California and Grandma Winburn's death, the problem became more acute for us children. Without Lois' interference, Dad had the upper hand. A generalized unrest and depression filled the house as we children connived to participate in the festivities that we saw all about us, and Dad's conscience bothered him for permitting as much Christmas spirit to enter our home as he did. Mother was always caught right in the middle, pleasing no one and resented on both sides for her attempts to compromise.

The year after Lois left we were told that an electric log in the fireplace had replaced the Christmas tree. That first year we were allowed to decorate the living room with evergreen branches, but after that no decorations were allowed. Mother provided a few presents, and we knew that Dad would come through with a five-dollar bill apiece about noon on Christmas Day, as his natural generosity overcame his holiday taboos. However the high point of December was the arrival of a huge box from California filled with beautifully wrapped gifts. Lois still managed to make sure we had a merry Christmas. At least Dad's scruples did not extend to the dinner table. He was always ready to appreciate good food, whatever the occasion. Mother's household economy was the only restraint on our preparation of holiday goodies.

After our marriage, Chad and I tried to emphasize the spiritual meaning of Christmas, playing down the material. After the children were born, we seriously attempted to celebrate the day as Jesus' birthday. Gifts were given to one another as an expression of the love we felt for the tiny baby who had come into the world to be our Savior. But another difficulty intruded into our lives to blast the serenity of the nativity. In Jean and Russell Stendal's Scandinavian heritage, the long, dark winter was enlivened and brightened by the Christmas season. They rejoiced not only in the birth of Christ, the Light of the world, but also in the return of the sun which had now passed the darkest point of the year and would be returning more and more each day. Jean had brought with her from Norway cherished memories of Christmas and while she was not much concerned with the spiritual significance, she entered heart and soul into the excitement of the holiday festivities. But to us, Chad's parents were the epitome of the materialistic concept of Christmas, which we deplored. Each year, as the presents piled up higher and higher around the Christmas tree, we determined to do things differently. However all we managed to do was to offend Chad's parents and spoil their enjoyment of Christmas with us, their only family.

In December, 1961, as I faced leaving our American culture and families and launching forth into a new life, I earnestly sought the Lord for the answer to the problem of Christmas. "This is supposed to be Your birthday, Lord Jesus. How would You like it celebrated?"

Now, a year later, as we faced actually departing for Jungle Camp, I incorporated the answer I felt the Lord had given me into a Christmas letter, nicely printed at Bethany on brown parchment-like paper with pinecones and red candles in the corners, and sent it to the mailing list that we had compiled of relatives and friends.

> "Have you ever caught yourself wondering what the Christmas rush, gaudy decorations, social events, and broken toys have to do with the birth of a Baby who was to be called the Son of God?

> "A year ago we asked this question: 'Lord, what would You like for Christmas, this day in which the world remembers Your birth?' The answer came quickly, and was so obvious we were surprised that we had never thought of it before. 'My great desire at Christmas or at any time is to be born anew in the hearts of those who will make room for Me.'

> "Many here in the United States have passed up this priceless treasure of Christ in you as unimportant; however there are millions of souls in the world who have never believed because they have never heard. **How shall they believe in him of whom they have not heard? And how shall they hear without a preacher?**

And how shall they preach, except they be sent?
(Romans 10:14-15)

"We praise the Lord that He has called us and is sending us to Colombia, South America, to share the news of Christ's birth, sinless life, and perfect atonement for sin with a tribe of people who have never heard."

As January drew to a close, and we prepared to turn the house over to the renters, I began to have second thoughts about going to Jungle Camp. Although I had recovered quickly from the acute stage of pneumonia, I still felt weak and got tired easily. My neck and left shoulder muscles were bothering me again. Some evenings I had to hold my head up with my left hand as I served supper with my right. I would soon be 33 years old (to me an advanced age), and I thought of the strong, healthy young people in their early twenties whom I had met in Grand Forks. They too would be attending Jungle Camp. How could I compete with them in physical endurance and activities? Once again I felt that I should never have gotten into this. I didn't even have the endurance to walk to the supermarket three blocks away and carry home a sack of groceries. How could I hike fifty miles? (We had heard second-year students at Grand Forks tell about the fifty-mile hike at Jungle Camp.)

As I brooded over this matter, a verse from Isaiah that I had memorized as a teenager came to mind: *But they that wait upon the Lord shall renew their strength; they shall mount up with wings as eagles; they shall run, and not be weary; and they shall walk, and not faint.* (Isaiah 40:31)

I looked up the reference in the Bible and was astounded to find that the verse directly before it read: *Even the youths shall faint and be weary, and the young men shall utterly fall.* Then I saw the verse prior to that one: *He giveth power to the faint and to them that have no might, he increaseth strength.*

Once again, my faith was renewed.

Chapter 5

On Our Way

Around the first of February we started out. Our Jungle Camp equipment – one duffle per adult and 1/2 duffle per child – was tied securely to a car-top carrier on the old Mercury. Our friends had been asked to pray that the Mercury would make it down to southern Mexico and back. Once again Grandpa Dick stood in the driveway and sadly waved us off.

In Texas we met the Walton's, Jim and Jan, with their two small children, Diana and Danny. Jim and Jan had been our classmates at the University of North Dakota, and we had decided that two old cars traveling together through Mexico would be safer than one old car alone. We stopped in Texas to visit a cousin of mine whose husband was in the U.S. military. He gave us a good supply of army 'C' rations. These 'C' rations supplied a picnic lunch for all of us for the several days it took to travel from the border to Mexico City. Our boys were very interested in the fact that each pack of 'C' rations contained a round can of cigarettes that we adults quickly threw away.

We made an effort to find clean, pleasant hotels, and I did not experience the culture shock I had felt on our previous trip across the border. Our trip to Mexico City to join our fellow Jungle Campers was uneventful except for an overheated radiator. Stopping at a service station, our meager Spanish vocabulary was increased by two new words: *caliente* (hot), and then as the attendant released our radiator cap, *muy caliente* (very hot).

In Mexico City, we found lodging in a small hotel conveniently located near the Wycliffe Headquarters, a large, castle-like building, affectionately nicknamed The Kettle. Desiring a shower after the dusty drive, I was chagrined to find no soap in the bathroom. Chad and the children had gone out on the street to look around, but I managed to contact the bell hop and requested *soapa*. I knew this sounded like a Spanish word. The bell hop shook his head doubtfully, staring at me like I was crazy. He pointed to his watch and tried to tell me something, but I just stood there saying *soapa*. Finally I gestured towards the bathroom, and a light went on in his head. In a few minutes he was back with a bar of soap. *Jabon* he gravely explained. Later on I found out that *sopa* was soup.

After a week or so of orientation lectures and sessions on Mexican culture and history, we all shoved off for *Tuxla Gutierrez* in the Mexican state of *Chiapas*, the jumping off point for Jungle Camp. The Walton family and our family decided to stay together again. However it always took us longer to get ready to travel each morning than it did the Walton's. I wondered if it was the additional child that slowed us up. Try as I might to get an early start, they always had to wait for us.

The first stretch of the trip from the Mexican capital to *Vera Cruz*, a pretty city on the Atlantic seacoast, involved crossing the continental divide at 10,000 ft. above sea level. Majestic, snow-capped peaks rose up on both sides of the highway. At one point we lost 2,000 ft. of altitude in eight miles. In one day, we traversed mountains, deserts, and jungle, and ended up at the seashore.

The next morning Chad and the children went for a swim in the ocean while I packed the car, and the Walton family waited patiently. This next stage of the journey took us from the coast to *Catemaco*, where we stayed at a lovely resort hotel beside a scenic lake. Several hours before our arrival at *Catemaco*, menacing black storm clouds arose directly in front of us, and a heavy headwind indicated that we were driving right into a sinister tropical storm. Expressing his alarm to us, Chad asked Chaddy to pray aloud as we all joined with him silently. Little Chad closed his eyes and started to pray. To our amazement, his concern seemed to be for the duffle bags on the top of the car. He asked God to please keep them from getting wet.

We continued on. Rain was falling now, to the right and to the left, but not a drop fell on the road, the car, nor the duffle bags. Just before dark, we arrived at a lovely hotel. As we stood on the balcony outside our room and looked back over the direction from which we had come, we saw the ugly black clouds, but right through the middle of them was a narrow strip of bright blue sky. To us it was a promise of future help and protection. God had answered Chaddy's request. The duffle bags had not gotten wet.

Leaving *Catemaco* the next morning, we came to within a few miles of the Pacific coast, then crossed another range of mountains to *Tuxtla Gutierrez*. Darkness fell while we were still in the mountains, and it was another new experience to navigate the narrow, twisting, mountain road in the dark, barely missing burros and cattle, which wandered about freely. Both Russell and Chad were suffering from diarrhea, and Russell was carsick as well. Remembering the song he had sung in the Minnesota woodlands, Chad led us in a revised version, *The Lord knows the way through the mountain road, All we have to do is follow.*

At last we arrived at the mission house at *Tuxtla*, where we were directed to a restaurant for supper. It was a beautiful place with formally dressed waiters. Chad immediately went in search of the men's room, and Russell indicated to me that he was going to vomit. Two empty coca cola glasses were sitting on the table, and I was able to catch the liquid in the glasses, filling them both to the brim. Now the problem was that of disposal. Chad returned and noted the problem. A white-jacketed waiter with a black bow tie had just served a meal to another table and was returning to the kitchen with an empty tray. As he passed our table, Chad stopped him and said, "*El nino* (the child), made a sign with his hands from his stomach to his mouth, and set the two glasses on the tray. The waiter gravely carried them out, and I almost died of embarrassment.

At the end of the meal, Russell repeated the performance, and once again, I neatly caught it in an empty glass. As the bill had been paid, we beat a hasty retreat. The Waltons were still sitting at a nearby table when the waiter appeared to clear our table. Seeing the full glass, he looked at them meaningfully, rolled his eyes, and rubbed his own stomach.

The next morning, all of us third session jungle campers congregated at the Missionary Aviation Fellowship mission house. This was a busy day for the MAF pilots. They would fly a plane load of third session campers to Main Base, then pick up a load of first session campers from Advance Base and bring them back to *Tuxtla*. These missionary candidates had now finished their jungle training and were picking up their cars and heading back to the United States. The second session campers had now finished their Main Base training and were on their long trek by trail to Advance Base. The Waltons and the Stendals were scheduled for the last flights, which would not leave for two days. Therefore we had time to visit with the hardy veterans of the first session who were beginning to arrive. It was reassuring to see that at least they had survived the experience. We were later to become well acquainted with many of these people in Colombia.

I was horrified to see that the legs of the women campers were covered with ugly, red insect bites, some of which looked to be infected. I certainly hoped that my legs wouldn't look like that in three months. All of the northbound campers seemed to be in high spirits and talked most positively about the training they had just completed. I still remember George DeVoucalla, who years later was our next door neighbor in Colombia, telling us how impressed he was with the leadership. "They start you out easy," he told us, "Then they add things gradually until you are doing things you never dreamed you could do."

After the first day in *Tuxtla*, I noticed that I had tiny red spots on my legs. It turned out that these were made by tiny black gnats. The next afternoon, we were taken to a zoological exhibit in a local park. While walking along a grassy path, I looked down at my legs. On each red spot sat a small black gnat busily biting through the scab and reopening the bite in order to suck more blood. Now I knew what had happened to the legs of the first session campers. Blood was already oozing out of several of the bites and attracting more gnats. I almost went into shock, not from blood loss, but from revulsion. Frantically, I brushed the gnats off my legs. I vowed to wear long pants from that moment on.

Chapter 6

An Unexpected Shock

At last it was our turn to climb into the little MAF plane. Soon Main Base came into sight. Picturesque thatched-roofed mud huts surrounded a large rustic building. Foot trails connected them all together. The camp was on a large knoll, and a winding river circled a portion of the lower part. We landed on the small strip, and a friendly missionary in a Texan hat opened the airplane door and welcomed us to Jungle Camp. It was March 1, 1963.

Two days later, I wrote to my mother in Minneapolis:

> *Jungle Camp is a beautiful place. It is built up on a hill and is cleared of underbrush except for pretty trees. The jungle is all around, but you don't feel like you are in it. We have a little mud hut with a high peaked thatched roof. Sharon and Chaddy have great big cribs, and the rest of us have beds built of bamboo. We sleep under mosquito nets, and it is much easier to keep the nets on the cribs. Chaddy felt too old for a crib at first, but now we call it a covered wagon, and he likes it just fine.*

To Genie Dean, my best friend from the prayer group, I wrote at 5:00 a.m. on March 6:

I'm going to try to write a few lines while waiting for someone to tell us how to "can a cow." One group killed it last night, and now the rest of us have to can it this morning.

We went on an overnight hike Monday night. The whole family went out and slept in jungle hammocks. Would you pray especially for the children? Russell has been sick ever since we got here – vomiting and diarrhea. So far medicine hasn't helped, although the doctor started him on something new yesterday, and he seems better.

The food here is very different from anything we have eaten before, and Sharon and Russell are having a hard time adjusting to it.

Someone must have arrived at that point to show us how to "can the cow" because the letter continues at 5:00 p.m.

Chad and all three children just went to visit a Tzeltal Indian village. They have a list of words to find like house, dress, blouse, etc. We were taught a few phrases like, "What is that?"

Tell Alice D. (the lady in charge of most social functions at Oxboro Church) that I am the crew chief of a cooking crew. None of the other four on my team have done any cooking before. Yesterday we made a chocolate cake, ten times the recipe. We used liquid shortening, didn't sift the flour (that is supposed to compensate for the liquid shortening). We looked in the oven every few minutes and took the cakes out and rotated them, but they all turned out fine.

I wish you could see our little mud hut. It's very cute, but we don't have time to be in it much. I learned to go down the rapids feet first on my back, using my hands as fins under my seat to keep from hitting my tailbone on a rock.

Our group butchered a cow last night and cut up and canned all the meat today. I didn't have to be at the butchering as I was baking the cake then. Keep praying for us all.

Love, Pat

That first overnight was a traumatic experience for me. Although a simple affair – we simply walked out into the woods after our last afternoon class, ate supper cooked by the staff, hung our jungle hammocks, slept all night, ate breakfast in the morning, and walked back to Main Base again in the morning in time for our first class session. The fact that I would have to sleep in a hammock scared me. Missionaries who had visited our home in the USA had told me it was a most uncomfortable experience. My neck and left shoulder were still aching, and I imagined that a night in a jungle hammock would greatly intensify the problem.

The other factor that distressed me was that the children had to go along. Four-year-old Sharon whined and fussed, and I had to carry her piggyback, even though the staff frowned and let it be known that they considered her old enough to walk.

As soon as we arrived at the camping area, I noticed the staff members scooping up water from the river in five-gallon cans to make soup for supper. The very idea of drinking water right out of the river made me feel sick. Later on, when we ate the soup in the semi-darkness, I was sure it was full of seaweed from the river. I later realized that the soup was a packaged Mexican variety with shredded dehydrated vegetables; however I ate very little supper that night.

The children went to bed nicely in their sleeping bags, which were placed inside the jungle hammocks. These hammocks were an invention of the U.S. Army for use in the South Pacific during World War II. They had a false bottom that prevented insect bites from below, a waterproof roof, and screening on the sides. One entered by means of a zipper that ran the length of the hammock underneath the net on one side. Once into the hammock, nestled within a sleeping bag, all was well so long as you lay quietly. A sudden movement, however, was likely to tip the entire hammock, and you would be lying on the netting with the zipper either under your body or up on the top. In either case it was necessary to attract the attention of a fellow camper or two to right your hammock again. In this type of emergency, it was also quite likely that the hammock would rip.

In the middle of this first night in the jungle, I woke up and saw Little Chaddy standing beside his hammock in the moonlight, looking rather dazed. I don't know how he got out, but I considered it quite an achievement when I finally managed to alight from my hammock. I zipped him back into his hammock and returned to my own again. In the morning, I discovered that Sharon was tipped sideways and had slept on the netting, however since she was so lightweight, and there had been no rain, it didn't matter. I just lifted her out the top.

Breakfast, also prepared by the staff, consisted of oatmeal, something I had avoided all my life, but this morning there was nothing else, and I had to admit it tasted pretty good. (I hadn't seen the staff making it out of river water.) As we walked back to the Main Base, I realized that the pain in my neck and shoulder was gone. Somehow I lost it that night in the jungle hammock. And now, almost fifty years later, it has never returned.

A bit tired and feeling more stress than usual, we gathered at 8:00 a.m. in the rustic, thatched-roofed dining room, the only large assembly room at Jungle Camp, for our class in general missionary orientation. Our director's opening announcement struck us like an electric shock. He had just received word of the death of two Wycliffe translators in Vietnam. They had been shot in full view of their families as they waited at a roadblock. A small child who was in her father's arms had also been shot. One of these martyrs was Elwood Jacobson, Vurnell's husband, my friend from childhood days. Our director went on to predict that as world conditions worsened, we should all be prepared to lay down our lives at any moment. We were all extremely saddened and shocked. After time spent in soul searching and prayer for the bereaved families, we filed out of the room, a silent, sober group.

Chapter 7

Main Base

The three months of Jungle Camp were divided into two six-week sections. The first part was held at Main Base. Here we learned what we would need to know to live in a primitive environment. Each family slept in a one-room mud hut, but meals were eaten all together in a large dining room and cooked by crews of campers using a large wood-burning stove. The dishes were washed and sterilized by crews of campers. A jungle school was held for the children of the campers, and a rustic nursery was provided for the younger children. Besides the general orientation, we had classes in health, sanitation, and basic medical treatment, care and use of camping equipment – camp stoves, lanterns, post-hole diggers, etc. We also had classes in carpentry, swimming, canoeing, mule-riding, and even an optional class in extracting teeth.

Hikes to neighboring villages of the Tzeltal Indians became progressively longer, culminating in a long three-day hike, in which we would cover 50 miles. All the while, staff members were watching and evaluating each camper. They wanted to pick up character or personality traits that if not overcome would make the person a liability to whatever mission group he was sent to work with.

The last six weeks would be spent at Advance Base. There each family unit would be on its own – building a house, cooking, and sleeping.   After the first week, daily classes would be held as well.   As the 50-mile hike was the big challenge of Main Base, the survival hike was the high point of Advance Base.   This was a simulated survival experience in which our physical and spiritual mettle would be put to the ultimate test.   We would each spend a night alone in the jungle, isolated, and without equipment.   It was this experience that we jungle campers both anticipated and dreaded.

At Main Base, the various Wycliffe fields, countries in which the mission was working, were presented for the consideration of the Jungle Campers.   We would be allowed to state several choices in order of preference, or we could leave our field assignment to the discretion of the board. Colombia was presented as a very difficult new field where only the top linguists would be assigned.   The first people assigned to Colombia had just entered the country, and the first scanty reports were just coming back.   My heart was touched to hear of tribes who were in slavery to other tribes in the southeastern jungle.

Since the Catholic Church was the official religious organization working in the tribal areas, some of the first linguistic teams were being placed on Catholic mission stations to begin their study.   At one point we were told that in Colombia, linguistic teams were being placed on a tribal boundary, and each member of the team had to learn and analyze a different language. I had visions of our family living on a Catholic mission station and Chad and I each studying a different language.   In view of my father's strong anti-Catholic feeling, I wondered how we would ever manage.

Then I remembered an incident from the University of North Dakota campus. Little Chad was out riding his tricycle on the sidewalk between our dormitory and a classroom building. A teaching nun in full black habit approached him on the path on her way to her summer session class. Chaddy stayed right in the middle of the narrow walkway. When the sister was squarely in front of him, Chaddy looked up at her with his big blue eyes full of wonder. "Are you Catholic?" he softly asked.

The sister looked for a moment at the little fellow with his chubby cheeks and ringlets of strawberry blond hair. "Yes, I am," she answered with a big smile, and then went on her way.

"Don't worry," Chad whispered in my ear, obviously remembering the same incident, "We'll let Little Chaddy charm them." I wondered how I would ever manage to handle a language all by myself and do a complete translation of the New Testament while Chad did another one, but we felt firmly committed to naming Colombia as our only choice of field assignment. Later in Colombia, we learned the truth behind the rumor. Two single men translators, living as temporary partners, had done just that. They lived on a Catholic Mission Station and each one studied a different language. Later they each married and continued the study together with their wives, just the same as any other married translation team.

On March 14th after two weeks of Jungle Camp, I wrote to Genie:

> *This is really the place for putting into practice all the theory of living the Christian life.*

The daily lectures on missionary medicine were obviously upsetting to me, as I continued in the same letter:

> *If it were not for the confidence that the Lord is going to take care of our health, I would just have to give up. We have a lecture every afternoon by the doctor, and all the things that can happen to you here are fantastic. The things that scare me most are malaria and snakebite. I wish you would especially pray for us in this regard.*

I was frustrated in my resolve to keep my legs covered to avoid insect bites. The Tzeltal Indians, in whose midst we were living, did not approve of pants on women. Also, in their culture straw hats were worn only by men. The

Jungle Camp staff had decided to allow us women to wear straw hats as our pale heads and faces desperately needed sun protection, but they decided to take a firm stand against women in pants.   When pants were required for certain activities, such as mule riding, they had to be hidden under a full skirt.   This was much too hot for everyday wear, and most of us felt too fat and round wearing so many layers of clothing.   I decided I had to just live with the bites.

I found that even with a straw hat and sunglasses, the direct glare of the tropical sun gave me a headache.   To make it worse, one of my duties was to hang several dozen white dishtowels on the clothesline at 1:00 p.m. and take them in after classes.   The bright midday sun glaring on the white towels gave me a sick headache for the rest of the afternoon.

During our morning group devotional time, we often sang a hymn based on Psalm 121.

> Unto the hills around do I lift up
>
> My longing eyes;
>
> Oh whence for me shall my salvation come,
>
> From whence arise?
>
> From God, the Lord, doth come my certain aid,
>
> From God, the Lord, who heav'n and
>
>   earth hath made.
>
> Jehovah is Himself the keeper true,
>
> Thy changeless shade;
>
> Jehovah thy defense on thy right hand
>
> Himself hath made.
>
> And thee no sun by day shall ever smite,
>
> No moon shall harm thee in the silent night.

(Charles H. Purday Hymnal of Intervarsity Christian Fellowship, Intervarsity Press, Chicago, IL)

This seemed to be the favorite hymn of whoever was making the selections.   Looking up the Psalm, I found these words: *The sun shall not smite you by day, nor the moon by night.* This seemed like a promise tailor-made for my situation. I began to actively exercise faith and claim the promise as my own. Little by little I noticed less trouble with the sun, until at last I found I was not aware of pain in my eyes and head anymore. Throughout the years in Colombia, I have been able to go out at midday with no protection and no discomfort. (I probably have a few more wrinkles as a result.)

After thanking Genie for the sunglasses she had given me, the letter continues:

> We are learning a lot of valuable things here. Both Chad and I can see that this course is just the right thing for us. Please pray for the children. Russell is having the hardest time adjusting physically. Chaddy is doing just fine physically but is extra cross and demanding. Sharon is cross and whiny around us but seems to be happy in the nursery. She is not eating well, but she was a poor eater at home too.
>
> The food is very strange here, but we are getting used to it. The whole concept of menu planning is eating to live, not for enjoyment. We have no bread or butter, little meat, and nothing fancy. Cakes never have icing, and we are just wild about them plain. Refrigeration is very limited, so we never have Jell-O or anything like that. I think I miss sweets the most of anything, but praise the Lord, I'm adjusting better than most people. I don't think I've lost any weight either. Too bad!

To my parents I wrote on March 18:

> All our drinking water has to be boiled, so we are getting used to drinking warm water. If we let it set overnight, it gets quite cold. We sterilize all cans before opening them and fresh fruit by immersing in boiling water for five seconds. All dishes must be scalded with boiling water. Once you get used to these things, it isn't so bad.

On April 1, I wrote again:

> *Chad has lost a lot of weight, but I haven't. We must have eaten pretty well at home, because some people here are raving about the food.*

To my sister Dorothe on April 4:

> *You just never know when you will have to do something all of a sudden that you never expected to do in your life. At times like that I feel such a calmness that I know it is because people are praying for me. Tuesday, I had to help skin a steer right while they were taking out the innards on the other side. It didn't really bother me. I got up at 4:30 a.m. and made baking powder cinnamon rolls, sixteen times the recipe.*
>
> *We have pretty good food here, but not at all what we are used to. For breakfast we have eggs, cooked cereal, and perhaps biscuits. For dinner we have some kind of main dish – meat or a casserole – and a vegetable. That is all, and sometimes it seems quite skimpy. For supper we might have soup, black beans and cornbread, or pancakes, and a dessert. We have tortillas or tostados, which are crisp tortillas.*

The clinic class was a daily trial. I felt the symptoms of each strange, tropical disease that we studied. Admittedly, our medical training was a drop in the bucket, but we were encouraged to do our best in the tribal situations, as whatever aid we could give would be better than nothing. I felt that the women with nurses' training in their backgrounds were head and shoulders above the rest of us. At least they were able to learn from the lectures and ask intelligent questions. We were all instructed in sterile technique and required to apply two intramuscular injections under supervision. I managed to survive all this, but when an optional class in tooth extraction was offered, I went out and took a long walk in the jungle.

Chapter 8

The Long Canoe Trip

After a series of lectures and sessions on handling dugout canoes and water safety, including how to go down rapids feet first, head raised, and with your hands protecting your tailbone from rocks, we were ready for our long canoe trip.

On the longer trips, the campers were divided into two sections. One section went on the trip one week, and the next week the trip was repeated for the other section. In the case of families with small children, each parent was assigned to a different section so that one parent would be able to stay at Main Base with the children. Some of the older children were allowed to go with their parents.

When the time for the long canoe trip came, Chad was assigned to the first group. This trip took place on a Saturday, a week before Easter. Since canoeing was an area of expertise for Chad (He had been the canoeing instructor at Pioneer Girls camp, and he had also taken groups of boys from our church on wilderness canoe trips in the boundary waters of northern Minnesota), he asked permission to take 7-year-old Russell along. The director of the camp whom we had known at the University of North Dakota gave permission, but the second in command of Jungle Camp, who would be in charge of this particular canoe trip, thought Russell was too young to go.

Chad's group was told that whoever got to the river first on the morning of the trip would have their pick of canoes. These were big, heavy dugout canoes holding four or five people. However one was a smaller canoe with a square stern. Seemingly one end had been cut off. It was now a 3 man canoe and very tippy. Although Chad and Russell were the first to arrive at the river that morning, they were told that if Russell were going to go, they had to take the tippy canoe. A large, awkward woman was assigned to sit in the bow with Chad steering and Russell in the middle. Chad thought that the leader was expecting the tippy canoe to capsize soon, and then hoped that Chad would send Russell back to Main Base.

However as they rounded the first curve about 200 yards down the river, there was the overturned canoe of the leader. He and his passengers were floundering in the water, as the swift river current swept Chad and Russell in the small canoe safely past. When they arrived at the stopping point for lunch, Chad noticed that all the other canoes were wet inside, indicating that they too had capsized. All the other canoeists were wet and disheveled, and some of the lunches had been carried away downstream. When they loaded up again to continue the trip, all of the women wanted to ride in Chad's canoe.

The second canoe trip to which I was assigned took place the next Saturday, the day before Easter. We started early, and I was assigned to the small canoe along with a newly married couple. In our canoe classes, we had been taught that no one was allowed to push a canoe from behind. This was considered to be a safety hazard as a canoe could be rammed into the legs of those who were pulling the canoe upstream by the tow rope. The other danger was that the canoe could get turned around and carried by the strong river current back downstream again.

Our trip downriver was great. The man, a strong, husky fellow who also had a lot of experience in canoeing, was steering in the stern, while his wife sat ready and alert in the bow with the other paddle to push us away from submerged logs, rocks, or other obstacles. I sat in the middle seat and enjoyed the ride.

I can't remember if anyone tipped over on our trip, and after our picnic lunch, we all started back upstream. All the occupants of each canoe lined up in front of their canoe, one behind the other, with the heavy tow rope over their left shoulders and proceeded to pull in unison to move the heavy canoes upstream against the strong current of the river. A space was left between canoes to provide safety in case of a problem. The three of us from the small canoe dutifully lined up to haul our canoe, plenty heavy although smaller than the others, up the river and back to Main Base.

This was very hard work, but we were making good progress until the man decided that he knew better than the instructors. He dropped the tow rope and went behind to push the canoe—the very thing we had been told not to do. Seeing this, the wife gave him a tongue lashing and told him to get back on the tow rope where he belonged. This he absolutely refused to do, so she threw down the rope in disgust and climbed the bank of the river.

I could have gone to the bank with the woman and left the ornery guy to manage the canoe alone, but since there was no one in sight either in front or behind, I decided that it was better to follow my instructions no matter what the others did. If the canoe turned tail and went downstream again, we would all three receive bad marks for the trip. So, I put the tow rope over my shoulder and pulled the canoe back to camp. It took all of my strength to keep the bow of the canoe pointed upstream. The man pushed from behind, and I must say that he was careful to keep up with my pace and not run me over.

Meanwhile the woman walked along the shore, berating her husband all the way, while he periodically ordered her to get back in the river and help me on the tow line. We neither passed nor were overtaken by other canoes, so our pace must have been about par for the course. The wife was a tall, athletic woman and would have been a great help on the tow line. After the canoe was safely docked, I made a bee line for our mud hut and collapsed in bed.

At this point in time, I was still a very timid person. Perhaps I should have scolded the man too, or at least insisted that

the woman help me on the tow line. As it was, I wore myself out. The next morning, I was so stiff and sore, I could hardly stand. I staggered over to the dining room for a delicious Easter morning breakfast. I was grateful that it was not my cooking team that had to get up at 4 a.m. to prepare the breakfast feast.

Chapter 9

The Big Hike

The big fifty-mile hike was coming right up. The staff had been preparing us by afternoon hikes to increasingly distant villages; however I felt far from ready. I tired faster than most people. Chad was assigned to the first group that would make the fifty-mile hike. After they left, those of us at home had three days to prepare a homecoming feast for them. So we were busy baking bread, killing chickens, and preparing a very special meal.

Although most of the mules were used for cargo, a few were provided with saddles for riding. The women hikers were allowed to ride one hour for every two hours that they walked. The first half of the trip, steadily uphill, was done in two stages. The first night they camped beside the trail, then arrived the next day at a *Lacondon* Indian village where a Wycliffe couple had been working for some twenty years. The *Lacondones* were a very primitive tribe, and the years of labor had not produced a single convert. Chad's group caught the Indians in the middle of a centuries-old ceremony honoring their 17 gods, represented by clay pots with projecting faces. Each family had a dugout canoe full of intoxicating liquor. It was a challenging situation for the group of aspiring missionaries.

The next day, Sunday, the campers hiked to a Christian *Tzeltal* village. The contrast was amazing. Here the village was neat, and the Christian Indians greeted them with smiles and handshakes. "Good afternoon, my Christian brother (or, sister)," they said as they eagerly ushered the tired Jungle Campers into the little thatch-roofed church. With the New Testament in their own language and their own elders, these Indians conduct their own church services. The Jungle Campers furnished the special music, singing several hymns that they had learned in the *Tzeltal* language at Main Base. Although the two groups shared no language in common, the Jungle Campers felt a unity of spirit with these Christian Indians that transcended the barriers of language and culture, so different from the atmosphere among the non-Christian *Lacondon* Indians.

The next morning at 3:00 a.m., the group rolled out of their jungle hammocks and after a quick breakfast started the long journey back to Main Base – 25 miles. They made it in time for the evening meal.

Those of us who were holding down the home front had the welcoming supper ready, and except for a skeleton crew who stayed in the kitchen, we were all lined up by the fence, looking down the trail, eager to welcome the returning hikers. A fellow camper, a graduate nurse with extensive experience, came up and leaned on the rail fence beside me, engaging me in conversation. "I'm very concerned for _____," she said, naming one of the girls who was in the returning group, "This trip really must have been tiring for her."

Having noticed that this girl walked with a marked limp, I agreed that it undoubtedly had been. "I just realized as I walked down here behind you," continued the nurse, "that you also have a congenital hip problem."

I was astounded. It had been a long time since anyone had commented on my peculiar walk. Several times in my childhood, doctors had examined my feet, but none of them had ever suggested a hip problem. I gave little heed to her words, but they remained in my mind.

All of a sudden, the first hikers came into view. Then, soon they were all there, laughing, talking, all trying to tell their experiences at once. As soon as Chad and I were alone, he looked at me seriously. "You'll never make it," he said, "They'll have to carry you back on a stretcher. Your only hope is to get on a mule and stay there. Many of the women are afraid of the mules and try to avoid their turns."

"But I'm one of those who is afraid of the mules," I demurred.

After dark Chad went out and caught a mule, he saddled it and gave me mule-riding lessons. He showed me how the mule would pass close to trees, trying to scrape me off, and how I had to kick against the tree with my foot and push the mule away. I was terrified.

At last the fateful day arrived. As part of our preparation for the ordeal, we had been told the pros and cons of the various types of footgear. I was especially concerned about my feet. I had suffered with a painful arch problem for years and had worn orthopedic shoes. I now had special arch supports to go inside my shoes.   This morning while the mules were being readied for the trip, I was in our sleeping hut frantically trying on different shoes.   Chad wanted me to wear my heavy leather hiking boots.   They would give me more protection but would be tiring and would have to be removed to ford the rivers.   At last I decided on my light-weight tennis shoes with my arch supports inside.   With blue jeans under a full gathered skirt, straw hat and sunglasses, I was ready to go.   Around each of our waists was an army web belt that held two U.S. Army surplus water canteens and a machete.

It was raining when we started out, and the trail was very muddy.   I slipped and slid, and as I had feared, was one of the slower ones.   The pacesetters, which included our staff members, stopped frequently to rest, but by the time we slower ones caught up, they were ready to start again, a fact that meant that we didn't get any rest.   At the first river, I took off my shoes and socks and waded across barefoot, a useless attempt to keep my feet dry for a while longer.   As I replaced my shoes on the other side, I discovered that my arch support for the right foot was missing.   I was frantic. I was sure I would never be able to complete the trip, let alone the rest of Jungle Camp, without my arch support. A woman staff member helped me search both sides of the river bank, but to no avail.   At last we had to go so we would not be left too far behind.   In desperation I committed my feet to the Lord for better or for worse.   I couldn't see the sense in wearing one arch support, so I put it in my carrying bag, and trusted the Lord for both feet.   The mules came at a short distance behind the walkers.   They now caught up to us, and the staff member decided that it was my turn to ride a mule.   I later described the trip in a letter to Genie:

I was scared to death of the mules to start with, but I got over that.   The mules don't like mud either and wanted to walk on the side of the trail. The trouble with that was that they kept trying to knock your legs against the trees and your head against overhanging limbs.   We rode up steep, muddy, slippery hills, and down even worse ones. We crossed rivers and jumped over logs and mud holes. I've seldom been so scared in my life...

We had pouring rain the first day in the morning and all night. It was quite a unique feeling to be all alone in a little hammock out in the jungle. The rain was pouring down with lightning and thunder flashing and roaring, but in my hammock, I was dry, safe and comfortable.

The *Lacondon* Indians impressed me greatly. Phil Baer, the Wycliffe missionary-linguist gave us a lecture on the history of the work with the *Lacondones* and took us to the village. Although the Baers had spent 20 years among them, these Indians were unresponsive. He told us of one young man, Antonio, who had seemed to be the first convert, but pressure from the tribal elders caused him to return his tablet and pencil. "I cannot be a Christian," he sadly told the Baers, "I will just have to go to hell." After that the Baers rarely saw Antonio. When they visited the village, he was not in sight.

Strangely enough, when Phil Baer led our group of Jungle Campers to the *Lacondon* village, only two men were there, and one was Antonio. I was fascinated with his strange appearance and sad story. Except for bangs, Antonio's long, black hair was uncut

and uncombed. He wore a knee-length dress-like garment of a colorless, heavy home-woven cloth. His young wife wore an additional skirt under the dress and braided her hair with feathers. For many days, I earnestly prayed for Antonio.

That evening we gathered at the Baer home and were delighted to hear that another contact had been made a short time before with another group of *Lacondones* who had been quite responsive. The next day we visited the Christian *Tzeltal* village, then on Monday morning we started back to Main Base.

It was a long trip back. A number of us women rotated on the riding animals. As the animals sensed that they were on the homeward trail, they quickened their pace and passed up all the walkers. It was hard to hold them back. For the last stretch I was on a large, white mare. When the Jungle Camp gate came into view, a woman beside me on a mule shouted, "Let's let them go!" and took off like lightning. My mare was right beside her mule, neck and neck.

Chad and the children were standing anxiously at the gate, hoping for the best. They could hardly believe their eyes when I arrived, the first one of the group, galloping up on a white horse. God had answered their prayers.

Chapter 10

Advance Base

At last the morning came when we were all awakened at 3:00 a.m. to prepare for the journey to Advance Base. By 6:15 a.m., after a substantial breakfast prepared by the staff, we were ready to leave. We Jungle Campers had now organized ourselves and elected a governing body. We were now led to Advance Base by our chosen leaders. No staff members would be with us on the trail. The staff would close Main Base for the season, and certain ones would be flown to Advance Base later in the day to give us our instruction there. Each of the children was assigned a riding animal for the entire trip. The adults were expected to walk except for mothers with very young children who could ride with their children.

Food had been issued several days before according to the family quota. It consisted of staples like rice, flour, sugar, dried beans, and powdered milk. It was packed first in plastic bags, and then in cloth bags of various sizes with drawstrings. We had been told to bring these with us, and the ladies in my prayer group had made ours. All this food, enough to last our family for six weeks, was packed in large bags and labeled with our name. This and the 3 1/2 duffle bags that were allowed our family had been sent on ahead on the pack mules.

This was another day when the airplane was kept extremely busy. As soon as the sun came up we could hear it high over the treetops. In addition to transporting staff members to Advance Base, the second session Jungle Campers and the rest of the Main Base staff were all being flown back to *Tuxtla*.

The 20-mile trip seemed endless. Our elected leaders did their best, but we missed the experienced staff members to whom we had looked for guidance and expert advice. About midway, the oldest woman in our group slipped and fell, seriously injuring her leg. By this time many of the adults were becoming very tired, and the injured woman needed a mount, so the children who were on the riding animals were forced to double up.

As we neared the site of the Advance Base, the trail led right through the middle of a *Tzeltal* Indian village. The villagers stared at us as we straggled along down their main street. I don't know what they were thinking, but as I peeked into the dark interiors of their mud houses, I was thinking, "I sure hope I don't have to eat or drink anything in one of these villages." Everything looked grimy, and I was sure the diseases we had studied in our clinic lectures at Main Base were rampant in this village. We finally arrived at Advance Base where we were greeted by the same staff members who had seen us off that morning. They had been flown over in the airplane and had supper waiting for us.

It had been a long day, and we were glad to crawl into our jungle hammocks. Everyone hung their hammocks in the trees near the place where we had been served supper. In the morning, each family would fan out to search for a house site. I had just gotten to sleep when I heard the most awful screams coming from Russell's hammock. I got over to him as quickly as I could get untangled from my sleeping bag and out through the zipper opening of my hammock.

He seemed to be having a nightmare. I calmed him as best I could and then went back to my hammock. I had just drifted off to sleep when the screams started again. All through the night this was repeated, disturbing the sleep of the entire camp, although at least the rest of them didn't have to drag their tired bodies out of their hammocks. It seemed that every time Russell felt the movement of the hammock, he thought he was back on the horse, and that it was tipping over.

The next Sunday, I found time to write to my parents:

Sunday after Easter

> *We arrived at Advance Base, and I wish you could see us. We have a site on a river. The river here, the Jatate, is much bigger than the one at Main Base, but right in front of our place it is shallow, so the kids can go swimming.*

> *This is virgin jungle with big trees and vines all over. The Waltons are 50 paces on our right, and a couple from Washington State is 50 paces on our left. We have the ridgepole of our house up and the corner posts dug. I got my temporary stove built. It is a trench in the ground with an iron stove plate on top and a tin can chimney at one end. It works fine. I baked a chocolate cake this morning before church at 10. I baked it in a frying pan on the stove plate with live coals on top of the lid to bake it on the top. I was amazed at how well it turned out.*

> *We had a 20-mile trip on the trail last Tuesday. Sharon rode a mule all the way. At the start, I rode with her, later we led her, and at the end she rode alone. Chaddy rode a mule half way, and then had to give it up as some of the adults needed to ride. Russell had a beautiful brown mare. Only a child could ride her as she had a saddle sore. At the end, Chaddy rode behind him on a blanket.*

> *We arrived at 5:30 or 6:00 p.m. We were hot, thirsty, and tired, but the children were good.*

During the first week at Advance Base (A.B.), we were left free from classes and assignments so that we could work on our houses. Chad had found the food to be inadequate for his needs at Main Base and during the last weeks had remarked to a staff member, "At least at A.B. I will get enough to eat, since I will have my own cook again."

"You're forgetting," replied the staff member, "that at A.B. your cook will turn into a house builder."

At Main Base, we had been taught to chop with a machete and build using vines instead of nails – all the primitive skills needed to build the simple, temporary shelter, called a "*champa.*" That first morning at Advance Base (A.B.) Chad informed me, "You devote yourself to turning out good meals, and I will build the house. I can't work if I don't eat." He had lost a lot of weight at Main Base, as had a number of the other men. The others were heavy to start with, but Chad had been thin all his life, and now he was really gaunt. On top of everything else, the diarrhea that he had picked up on the trip down through Mexico was still bothering him. I knew that he needed good meals.

I reviewed my resources. In addition to the food we had been issued at Main Base, we were also each given a *Jungle Camp Cook Book*. This little book was filled with intriguing recipes that could be made with the ingredients available to us. In addition to the basics, we had also been issued a can of Crisco, peanuts, raisins, some cans of fruit and vegetables, and I believe there was some processed cheese and a can of crackers. The Jungle Camp director's wife had told us to be sure to use some of our "goodies" the first few days to tide us over the rough period of setting up our campsite, and then to save some for the end when we would be busy packing. In between we would have more time to "make things from scratch."

That first morning, we were also issued our kitchen equipment. Each family received a medium-sized wooden box that could be set up as a kitchen cupboard. It had a hinged door that when closed at night was practically insect proof. Inside I found five each of cups, bowls, soup plates, knives, forks, and spoons. There was also a large iron frying pan, four blue enameled cooking pots of different sizes, a pancake turner, and a large serving spoon. We were also issued a pressure cooker, several aluminum buckets and basins, and a stove plate. I went to work digging a trench for my temporary stove while Chad and the boys, machetes in hand, went to look for poles for the house. (A more permanent mud stove would later be built inside the house.) Chaddy, though only five, had been loaned a certain small machete called a "Woodsman's Pal." Chad had brought it in his duffle bag and considered it safer than the Jungle Camp machetes. He told Chaddy he could use it until he cut himself; then he would have to give it up. Sharon gathered sticks for firewood.

When we first arrived at A.B., Chad and I had a talk with the children. We explained that we were in a survival situation to see if our family could work together and do a good enough job to be allowed go to Colombia. We needed to have each one of the children make a contribution. They all rose to the challenge.

By noon I had a lunch of sorts ready. The ground sloped up away from the stove, and the three children sat on the dry grass, each with a little round bowl and a spoon. When they held out their bowls as I dished rice to them, I was reminded of a World Vision photo I had seen of Korean orphans with their bowls outstretched.

We had been instructed to keep our area sanitary. All waste and garbage was to be placed in a posthole and covered with earth. Chad hiked to the Center and borrowed a posthole digger. In the afternoon, he dug our posthole in an area where the heavy brush would give us privacy, and I set up a basin on a lashed tripod of poles and hung up a towel. Our bathroom was complete.

At the end of our first week at A.B., our house was still far from finished, but we had to start daily classes and continue construction in our spare time. We were still cooking on the temporary stove and sleeping in the jungle hammocks, but we now had a house with a roof – half thatch and half heavy plastic that we had been told to bring with us from the States, a table and benches. We lacked beds and the permanent mud stove, but we ate seated around the table, and the children no longer looked like little orphans with their rice bowls.

Five-year-old Chaddy loved working with his machete, the Woodsman's Pal. One day we came home from class and found that all the bushes that gave us privacy around our posthole were gone. On another occasion, Chaddy came up and whispered in my ear, "I'm going to show you something, but don't tell Daddy." Carefully he withdrew his hand from under his tee shirt and stuck a bloody little finger up in my face. His finger was cut to the bone, his first accident with the machete. Automatically I screamed for Chad, and we disinfected and treated the wound. It healed perfectly, and in a few days, Chaddy was happily chopping with the Woodsman's Pal again.

At Advance Base the afternoon classes in canoeing and swimming were optional for mothers with small children.

As I had quite a bit of experience in these two activities, I elected to stay at home with the children. There was no childcare at A.B. Russell went to school in the morning, but we had to take Sharon to class with us while Chaddy roamed freely in the jungle.

We had been given a list of books that were required reading, and we were asked to keep track of any other books we read from the camp library. We were also assigned a research paper on an approved subject. Chad with his engineering background chose to map the area of Advance Base. I wrote mine on the emotional adjustment of children to Jungle Camp. There was some material on file in the library, and I gained much data by interviewing all the mothers in my session. By this time I had finished all the required reading as I had been able to maintain my life-long habit of always keeping a book at hand to read in odd moments. However there were still a number of books in the Jungle Camp library that I wished to read before camp was over. I devoted myself to these pursuits in the afternoons while Sharon napped and the boys swam in the river.

One interesting detail of our life at A.B. was that we were asked to jot down in a notebook how we spent our time, accounting for every minute in segments of five minutes or more. All the activities were boiled down to "living" or "ministry." A person had to be able to organize their life so that a certain percentage of their time fell into the "ministry" column, or they were considered to be a poor prospect for the mission field. Luckily for me, reading and family devotions all fell into the "ministry" column. As we had lengthy family devotions each day, Chad and I excelled in the time devoted to "ministry." These afternoons gave me much time in the "ministry" column.

I took a long time in meal preparation and clean up, and of course that had to go into the "living" column. The Walton family was our nearest neighbor. We would all come back from morning classes at about the same time and start preparing our noonday meal. The Waltons always started off their mealtime by singing "Jesus Loves Me" with their small children one and two years of age. I had a private competition going on in my head to get our noon meal ready before the Waltons started singing. However try as I might, before I was ready to call my family to the table, I would hear "Jesus Loves Me" from the next champa. I don't think I ever beat Jan Walton.

At first our meals were limited to the provisions that had been issued to us at Main Base, but one day a cry went up and was passed from champa to champa, "One person from each champa to the center with a basin or pail." Produce had been purchased from the Tzeltal Indians who lived nearby and was divided among us campers according to the quota. Sometimes it was eggs, another time bananas or plantains, or another exotic jungle fruit or vegetable. One morning we received twelve pounds of beef and eight pint canning jars. I filled the jars with cubes of beef and processed them four at a time in my small pressure cooker. We smoked some meat, dried some, and ate all we could hold. For once in his life, Chad got all the meat he could eat.

Chapter 11

Russell and the Sugar Creek Gang

From time to time we saw members of the *Tzeltal* tribe, the indigenous group that lived in the Jungle Camp area. Women with colorful skirts and blouses and ribbons braided into their hair came to pick up our clothes to wash in the river. Our clothes were counted and tied in bundles by dozens and placed in a designated area together with a bar of soap and a certain amount of Mexican pesos. The clothes would be returned spotlessly clean, and we would hang them up to dry. Sometimes an Indian man was hired to work around Jungle Camp. Sometimes Indians came to the clinic for treatment or to sell their produce at the Jungle Camp store. Some spoke some Spanish, but since we didn't, that wasn't much help. We had learned a few words of their language at Main Base, and the children could sing several songs in *Tzeltal*, but once again, as I had in Mexico years before, I experienced extreme frustration at the inability to communicate. We were encouraged to make friends with the Indians, and Jan and I managed to have a friendship with a woman named Esperanza.

For our dealings with the Indians, we were encouraged to adopt Spanish names. Patricia was fine for me. Chad decided to use his middle name, Martin, which with only an accent change and a small difference in the last vowel would make a good, pronounceable name for the *Tzeltals* as well as the Latin Americans. As Russell was also a name not used south of the border, he too would use his middle name and be known as Martincito. Sharon Rose became Rosita. These names all stuck and have been used all our years in Colombia. Chaddy presented the problem. He finally said, "Just call me Alberto." In Colombia, however, Alberto has been forgotten. The Colombians have learned to say, "Chaddy," only changing the spelling to Cheri.

One day Jan and I and our children visited Esperanza in her village. Conversation lagged, but smiles were exchanged on all sides. The children helped out by singing "Jesus Loves Me" in the *Tzeltal* language. "*Mucho gusto, mucho gusto,*" responded Esperanza. I had no idea what she was saying, but Jan interpreted it for me as meaning, "Not much

gusto." Actually after learning some Spanish in Colombia, we realized she had said, "It pleases me very much."

One of our assignments at A.B. was clinic duty. At Main Base the doctor was in charge of the clinic, but here at A.B. we no longer had him to depend on. All the staff members, whether medically trained or not, were considered capable of handling the clinic. I admired their competence and that of the women in our group who had received nurses' training. In spite of our clinic classes at Main Base, I felt woefully incompetent in the clinic. I was especially terrified by the thought of giving injections and hoped no one would need one while I was on duty.

Russell was swimming like a fish in the river. One day he showed me some boils on his legs. I opened them, drained the puss, and disinfected them, but the next day the boils were worse. Chad said I had better take him to the clinic. The lady on duty was one of the Advance Base staff members. She prescribed penicillin shots. "It will be good practice for you to give them yourself," she smilingly but firmly stated. I saw no escape. The first one, given under the woman's supervision, went all right. Russell took it in stride. But the next day, when we went back for the next one, I was on my own. Russell was not as calm as he was the day before. "Please be brave," I begged. "If you don't fuss, I'll buy you a *Sugar Creek Gang* book when we get back to Minneapolis.

I inserted the needle, but the plunger would not go down. The needle was jammed. (These were glass syringes with needles that had to be sterilized and used over and over again. The needles got dull, and these at Advanced Base seemed to be blocked. By the time we got to our tribe in Colombia, disposable needles and syringes were in use.) I pulled out the needle, transferred the penicillin to another syringe and needle, and returned to Russell who by now had decided that he definitely did not want another shot. By promising him another *Sugar Creek Gang* book, I got another chance. Again, the same thing happened.

At last we walked home, Russell with a sore behind, but with the promise of not one, two, nor three, but four new *Sugar Creek Gang* books.

Chapter 12

Survival Hike

Our morning lectures had prepared us for the big event of Advance Base, the survival hike. The day was drawing near. All women campers were on the alert. At any moment we could be called out on survival. We got used to carrying our survival kit, water canteens, and matches whenever we left our houses.

To my chagrin, my left knee started aching, the same one that had been operated on after the bicycle accident years before. I mentioned this fact at the clinic, but no one had a solution. (Later, a doctor told me it was from walking over uneven ground.) On Wednesday at 11:00 a.m., the call came: "All women campers to the Center." I grabbed a sweatshirt and slipped a pair of jeans under my skirt.

After a short canoe trip, our guides led us around in the jungle awhile and finally brought us to a sandy beach by the river. We were told that a canoe had overturned, and we were survivors. We were to each set up a shelter and sleep on the beach at least 50 paces from our nearest neighbor. We were not allowed flashlights, plastic tarps, or any kind of food. All we were allowed of our survival gear was a machete and matches. Of course we always wore our web belts with two army canteens and their attached cups, one on each hip.

I started building my shelter by cutting down some small trees to use. I planned to build a nice big one on the sand, but it kept falling down. After the third attempt, I was really discouraged. The next time my shelter decided to stay up, but I had cut it down to half its original size. Thunder was rumbling and dark clouds threatened. I thatched my little shelter with branches and leaves from the trees I had cut; however I knew my shelter was far from rain proof.   I heaped up dry sand and laid some willow branches on top for a bed. Then I gathered firewood. I was beginning to feel very hungry, since we had eaten nothing since breakfast. After dark, four of us gathered at one girl's shelter. We were all drinking hot water from our aluminum canteen cups to fill up our empty stomachs. We gathered some green papaya and some purple leaves that were supposed to be edible, but I decided I wasn't hungry enough for that yet. After a bit we returned to our individual shelters for the night. Using my straw hat as a pillow, I slept surprisingly well, only waking up frequently to put more wood on the fire when I felt cold. The storm that had threatened must have gone another direction, as no rain fell during our time on survival hike.

We had been taught at Main Base to boil the river water for 5 minutes to kill the bacteria and parasites. The next morning we boiled water in our canteens and waited. Boiling water was one of our important activities on this survival hike. We boiled it right in our metal canteens over a large fire that someone had built on the beach. We all had quite a time finding a spot where we could balance our canteen in an upright position and then retrieve it again after it had boiled for 5 minutes without tipping it over and spilling the precious boiled water. Of course by now we were somewhat experienced at this from our other hikes and trips. Then the cooling process began. One way was to wade out into the river and cool the hot canteen in the cool, flowing water. The other was just to wait until the next morning when the water would be cooler than lukewarm. The important tip given during our training was STAY AHEAD. We each carried two canteens, and the trick was to get one boiled while the other one still contained cool water. Those who ran out or spilled their water had to drink warm or lukewarm liquid.

About 10:00 a.m. a canoe arrived from camp with our already prepared survival food, flashlights, and tarps. We were each given a special treat of two candy bars. Our survival food consisted of "snuff" (short for "it's enough"). This was a mixture of dry oatmeal, cornmeal, powdered milk, and shaved panela (a crude brown sugar). Our survival food also included raisins, dried smoked meat, and big chunks of panela. I washed the "snuff" down with lukewarm water and ate some raisins, but the smoked meat seemed too uncooked to be appealing.

At 11:15 a.m., the second part of the survival experience started. A list of names was read (those who were considered to be the most able-bodied, we found out later), and these women were marched off with one staff member. The other staff member took the rest of us off in the other direction. After trying to get us lost by leading us around in large circles, at last he brought us into a clearing, pulled an envelope from his pocket, and read us our instructions. We were the survivors of an airplane crash. Two of us, another girl and I, were pronounced to have broken legs. (We were picked for this because we had both complained at the clinic of pains in our legs.) The staff member was to be treated as an Indian whose language we didn't know. A search party (the other half of our group) was looking for us. As soon as we were found, our survival experience would be over. We could go back to Advance Base.

There were nine of us in the group of survivors. We elected a leader, and she sent four girls out to blaze base lines on the points of the compass to aid in our rescue. Since two of us were injured and couldn't work, that left only three to bring the firewood and prepare the sleeping places for nine people. The two women who were left to do this work together with the leader were the most fatigued of all of us. I felt terrible to be lying idle while so much work needed to be done. I started to chop wood, hopping on one foot, but the staff member reprimanded me. I finally chopped what I could while sitting down.

After the firewood was ready, the tired girls turned to bed making. The prospect of making nine beds was daunting, so they got the idea of just making one big bed for all of us. We were away from the sandy beach where we had spent the first night, and the ground had to be cleared of brush, rocks, and other debris. Then a frame needed to be built with cross pieces to get us all up from the ground out of the dampness, insects, and possibly snakes. Then in an effort to make it comfortable, the whole thing needed to be covered with small branches and twigs. Of course this was all supposed to be under a thatched roof, but the night was clear, and no one even mentioned that detail. We were still in the dry season. At least no one had to cook supper. Each one was on her own, eating her survival food. It started to get dark, and the trailblazers returned. They were very tired and reported that cutting base lines sounded easy in class, but was actually quite difficult. Some of them needed urgently to boil water and set upon that task. Some had gathered snails and decided to make snail soup in their canteen cups. Others had some purple leaves that we had been told were edible. We all ate more "snuff." Some boiled it in their canteen cups and ate it like cooked cereal.

Our "monolingual Indian" guide came over from his shelter, a stone's throw away, to see how we were doing. He looked at the bed and shook his head. He cut a few more cross supports for it.   Just as he headed back to his own place, a scream broke the silence. In her attempt to remove her canteen from the fire, one of the trailblazers had spilled water from her boiling hot canteen on her hand. As we all froze in horror, one girl, Joy, grabbed her own canteen of precious cool water and poured it all on the burned hand. (We had been taught in clinic class that a burn should be put into cold water as quickly as possible.) Now we had a real injury. I asked the "Indian" if I could trade places with the girl who was burned and let her be the one with the broken leg. He gravely nodded affirmative, so I was rid of my disability.

Two of the trailblazers looked at the bed and declared that they would rather sleep on the bare ground. That left seven of us to crawl onto the bed amid much complaining. Soon another girl left to sleep on the ground. Then we were six. One of the bed builders was the most vocal in her complaints. "You made this bed; now you have to sleep in it," one of the trailblazers called from her place on the ground. This gave us all a good laugh.

The bed was terribly uncomfortable. A forked stick, one of the supports of the bed, was under my head. I covered it with my straw hat and tried to go to sleep. Sometime in the night the bed went down, so we all finished the night on the ground.

The next morning we ate more "snuff." Our canteens of water were giving out now; especially Joy and the girl who had spilled her canteen of boiled water were very low. We had no source of water nearby. I was appointed as a trailblazer and went off with a companion to blaze a base line. Each team of trailblazers needed a watch to use together with the sun to keep on a straight line. Someone borrowed Joy's watch. Two girls found the river about 10 minutes walk away from our camp. That was a cause for great rejoicing, and all the girls left in camp hurried to wash up a bit and fill their empty canteens. Somehow the girl who had borrowed Joy's watch dropped it in the river. The watch was retrieved, but its days of usefulness were over.

Blazing was very hard work.   We despaired of ever making these lines long enough that the searchers would come across our blazes and be led into our camp. We all gathered dejectedly back at our campsite to rest. I decided to go to the river, and Joy accompanied me. Someone had told me what had happened to her watch, and I expressed my sympathy. It would be hard to get through the last weeks of Jungle Camp without a watch. I was surprised by her cheerful and magnanimous reaction. It was obvious that she held no ill will toward the girl who had borrowed it. Some of the other girls joined us at the river. One girl expressed the opinion that men do things like blaze base lines. Women just scream for help. We all stood up and screamed at the top of our lungs. Nine female voices can make quite a racket. We were pleased with ourselves and decided to repeat the performance every twenty minutes. After awhile a girl named Gail and I decided to go to the river. We met the searching party on the way. They had heard our shouts.

After carrying the two "injured" on improvised stretchers to the river, we were free to return to A.B. if we could find it. One of the women in the search party led us right to the main trail that we had used in our trip to A.B. some weeks before. Now we were really homeward bound. One of the single ladies mentioned that she knew that the staff was preparing a welcome home party for all the single women. "How about the married ones?" I asked. "Oh, your husbands will have a special meal ready for you," she replied. My heart sank. I knew that Chad had been having his own sort of survival training taking care of the three children for three days. I was just hoping they had all survived, and I didn't expect any kind of special reception. Still, I was so hungry and so tired, and the thought of arriving to find all the dishes dirty and nothing prepared to eat made me feel very sorry for myself. The more I thought of the singles' homecoming party, the hungrier and sadder I became. Finally I turned to the Lord, "Please, Lord, provide me something decent to eat," I pleaded.

The trail took a turn, and we passed right through an Indian village, the same one I had been so repelled by on our way to A.B. Only this time the street was deserted and the houses were empty. After passing through the empty village, we came to the river. Here were all the villagers gathered on the riverbank just upstream from the crossing. They were dressed in their best. The ladies wore colorful skirts and blouses, and the men spotless white shirts and dark trousers. It looked like they were having a picnic as they had carried tables and chairs from their houses. I was near the head of the group of dingy, grimy survivors as we dragged our weary bodies across the shallow ford of the river. Somehow I just hated to leave that happy group by the river. All of a sudden a shout rang out. Our staff member wanted us to stop. It seemed that the Indians had invited us to join their party.

We splashed back across the river again with a spring in our step. The Indians had us sit on blankets spread on the ground, and the Indian women brought us steaming cups of strong, hot coffee sweetened with panela, their homemade brown sugar. They also served us crisp, sweetened tortillas, a kind that I have never seen before or since. They reminded me of the Norwegian *krumkoke* that my mother-in-law used to serve each Christmas. I thoroughly enjoyed every bite and every sip of coffee. When we went on our way again, it was with a renewed spirit. I remembered my prayer of a few minutes before. "Thank you, Lord," I cried from my heart. Once again, the same Lord who had provided a birthday cake with just the right colors for a little girl in the middle of North Dakota had provided a special treat for a tired and disgruntled missionary candidate right in the middle of the Mexican jungle.

Arriving back at our *champa*, I found Chad and the children taking a swim. Russell had made pancakes for breakfast – three times the recipe. I wondered how a second grader could multiply fractions, but he explained that he had just measured each ingredient three times. He had used the largest cooking pot as a mixing bowl. As I had imagined, all the dishes were dirty. Chad and the children thought they had solved that problem creatively. They had piled all the dishes into the big kettle, tied it near the shore of the river, and submerged it in the water. There the small fish were busily nibbling at the food that still stuck to the dishes and cooking pan. They thought they were quite smart having the fish clean the dishes while they went swimming.

I went for a refreshing swim myself, and then dressed in clean clothes, I washed the dishes and fixed a good dinner. Chad did have a welcome home present for me. While I was gone, he had built a wonderful adobe mud stove inside our *champa*. Complete with chimney and a five-gallon can built in to heat water, it worked beautifully. No more cooking on the ground.

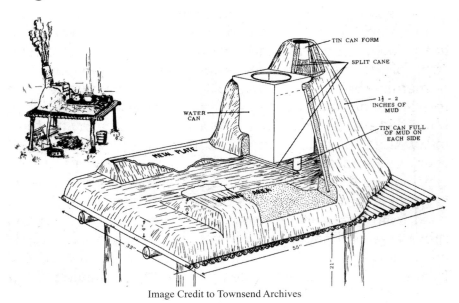

Image Credit to Townsend Archives

Chapter 13

Village Visits

Next on the schedule was our village overnights. Chad and Russell went to a *Tzeltal* village named *Abeblenal* and spent the night on a straw mat in an Indian home. When they returned, I was all ready to go with a girl named Audrey to a town called La Victoria. Audrey was a medical laboratory technician and an expert in giving shots. This was a good thing as the purpose of the trip was to administer the third DPT shot

to some 50 Indian children. An Indian family took us in for the night. The parents gave us their bed and slept on a mat by the fire.

This was the most uncomfortable night of my life, as the bed was made of hard, round poles lashed together, the head end higher than the foot.   However the Indian family was friendly and hospitable and gave us tortillas and eggs for breakfast before we left to return to Advance Base.   I was very frustrated by not being able to talk with them.

By now we were moving into our *champa.*   Using lashed poles, Chad built a second floor under the peak of the roof. The boys had an upstairs room where they spread their air mattresses and sleeping bags.   Since our days were very full, Chad had only evenings to build our beds.   One night about 9:00 p.m., he finished our double bed.   Now only Sharon remained outside in a jungle hammock.   When she realized that, she was heartbroken.   All of us were in the house, and only she was left outside.   Chad's heart was touched.   He went out in the dark to cut down trees, and although Sharon went to sleep in the hammock outside, she woke up inside the house in her own little bed.

The men eventually went on their own survival hike, and I was left alone with the children for three or four days. Getting firewood was the big problem. All the readily available dry wood near our campsite had been used. We now had to go away from camp to find fuel. Chad told me about a clearing where the Indians had chopped wood. Quite a few large chips had been left, which would serve to cook our meals while the men were gone, so I took the children and all the buckets, and we brought back a good supply. The first trip had been fun, but the next day when I tried to get the boys to go to the clearing again, they didn't want to go. Usually Chad enforced the discipline, but in my desperation at having to handle everything alone, I spanked them and sent the two little boys, five and seven years old down the trail crying with a bucket in each hand. They looked very small and pathetic, but they soon came back with their buckets full of chips. They preferred playing in the river with the small balsa rafts that they had made or cooking snail and rice soup over their own small fires. Sharon spent much of her time on a swing that Chad hung from a large branch on the bank overlooking the river.

The men were gone a little longer than we had been. They actually cut the base lines, and they had many adventures as well. Chad had the honor of being chosen the leader. I was very glad when the word passed from *champa* to *champa* that the men were coming home and happily prepared a homecoming feast.

Advance Base was almost to an end, and we still had not taken our family overnight canoe trip. It could be delayed no longer. We packed the jungle hammocks, sleeping bags, and food for supper and breakfast into a dugout canoe and took off. We found a pleasant, grassy area by the river about 20 minutes upstream and set up camp. Since our arrival at jungle camp the weather had been dry, but during that night the first downpour of the rainy season descended upon us.

About midnight, I detected above the raging tumult of the storm, a frantic screaming. During a short lull in the downpour, I was able to tell that it came from the bank near the river where Russell had pitched his jungle hammock. Rain was being driven by the wind into one end of his hammock through the mosquito netting, and he was dreaming that the river had risen and was flowing through his hammock. During another lull in the storm, I was able to attract his attention, and he came streaking over to my hammock, a little drenched and shivering figure. I tried to keep the hammock balanced, but as he climbed in I lost control, and we both fell into the netting on the other side of the zipper. The opening was now on top. After being aroused by our screams, Chad had to get up and go out into the downpour and balance us in the hammock again. I unzipped my sleeping bag and got Russell in with his head sticking out the bottom. We lay very quietly until daylight when I got up, managed to get a fire started, and cooked oatmeal. We had fulfilled the requirement – cook supper, sleep, and cook breakfast. Then we packed up and floated downriver to A.B. again. On my way back, I discovered that my wristwatch had stopped during the night, never to run again. Returning to the champa, we found that it had held up in the storm quite well, only the spot upstairs where Russell usually slept had been drenched.

Now we were in the last week of Advance Base. We were called in by the staff for our final evaluation, and to our great relief found out that we had passed the course. (Most did, but there were a few exceptions, such as the couple that were my companions on the canoe trip.) We left most of our clothes to be given away to the Indians, and while going through our gear, I found my arch support that I thought had been lost in the river. It had been left in one of my hiking boots when I tried them on the morning of the big hike before I opted for the tennis shoes. By then my arches were fine, and I haven't worn arch supports since.

On our last morning at Jungle Camp, Chad and Russell floated down the river to the airstrip on large balsa rafts made by the jungle campers, while the younger children and I went in a motor-powered dugout canoe. After the little airplane landed us in Tuxla, we were soon in our Mercury, heading north for Mexico City. This time we didn't bother with tourist hotels. We slept in little *residencias* that would never come close to appearing in an AAA directory. The Waltons went on ahead. I'm sure they made much better time without having to wait for us. None of us were so worried now about our cars breaking down in Mexico. After Jungle Camp, the lower class Mexican tourist accommodations were no longer threatening, they actually seemed luxurious. We ate tortillas, beans, and scrambled eggs in the inexpensive Mexican restaurants along the highway.

Somewhere in Mexico we spent the night with a Wycliffe missionary couple who were doing a translation for a tribe, and lived in a small town. Before going to the missionaries' home we visited the town plaza where a few venders were displaying their wares. We got a typical Mexican skirt for me and a matching shirt for Chad among a few other purchases. We bargained using our slowly increasing Spanish vocabulary and felt that we had gotten incredibly favorable prices. Later at the missionaries' home, we displayed our treasures and expected to be congratulated on our wonderful bargaining skills. To our surprise and consternation, the missionary man kindly reprimanded us. "Do you realize that you purchased these items at below the cost to the Indian family? They must have had no food for supper and no money, so they let you have their wares at below cost."

Chad and I felt terrible. There was nothing we could do about the present situation, but this has been a lesson to us for all the rest of our years in Latin America. We have never been such hard bargainers. We have always tried to make sure that the seller, as well as we, the buyers, got a good deal.

After taking a few days for car repairs in Mexico City, we headed for the U.S. border and Minneapolis. As we left Mexico City, Russell and Sharon sat in the front with Chad, and Chaddy and I sat in the back seat along with a huge birthday cake. It was a very beautifully decorated cake all safely packed in a box. We had purchased it in a bakery in Mexico City and planned to stop down the road a ways and celebrate Chaddy's sixth birthday.

Leaving Mexico City, the broad paved multilane highway descended some 2,000 ft. in well-engineered curves. For some reason Chad put the old stick shift transmission in neutral and let the vehicle coast, gathering speed all the way. Russell and Sharon thought this was great fun and urged him on, while Chaddy and I, who were terrified, hugged each other and begged him to slow down.

Egged on by his front seat passengers, Chad just grinned and whirled around the curves like a roller coaster. Chaddy and I were almost hysterical by the time we came to the plain and settled down to a normal speed. When we recovered our wits, we discovered that in all the excitement, I had sat on the cake and smashed it.

Jungle Camp must have been a success. The last night of our trip, as the money was very low, Chad and I unrolled our sleeping bags and slept on the ground in a park in Iowa while the children snoozed in the car.

At the Minneapolis city limits, Chad gave a cry, "I've lost my oil pressure!" It was the end for the poor old Mercury. It had carried us safely for some 3,000 miles through snowstorms, deserts and mountains, but now it was finished. We limped into a service station where the mechanics found that six different items had worn out. We called Dad, and he came and took us to a big welcome at 4440 Bryant Avenue. "We shouldn't have asked people just to pray that it would make it to Mexico and back, but that it would drive around awhile after we got here," commented Chad.

Chapter 14

Grand Forks Again

Grand Forks, North Dakota
    Summer, 1963

In a few days, the Lord provided a good deal on a used car. My parents bought it for us, and we were on our way to Grand Forks. This time we traveled light. We had learned that we could get along with much less stuff. Upon our arrival, we were excited to find a number of friends from our first year linguistic course and others from Jungle Camp enrolled in the second year class. Many of the staff were also familiar and gave us a warm welcome. We were happy to see that our friend, John, was in our class as well as the Waltons and Joy and Audrey from Jungle Camp. The children too found friends from the year before. Russell was soon engaged in a game of chess with the Longacre boys, children of one of our instructors. Instead of the difficult arrival of the year before, it was like returning home.

This time we had two large rooms on the first floor. I found that the first hour of the class schedule was my study time. The next hour was chapel, and then we were "off to the races" so to speak, because if we thought first year was difficult, second year was really hard. "I've never been in a place before where if I dropped my pencil, I found myself a week behind," mumbled Chad. One of our sessions was devoted to phonology, the sound system. After a short break, a session of tagmemic grammar with Dr. Longacre followed. Dr. Longacre was one of the pioneers of the tagmemic model of grammar analysis. This theory, first developed by Dr. Kenneth Pike, had enabled the Summer Institute of Linguistics to analyze the grammars of many dozens of Indian languages in many different parts of the world.

These two courses were extremely difficult and assumed that we remembered 100% of our first year studies. Since my free hour for study was the first hour of the day between breakfast and chapel, I decided that I was up against a hopeless situation, and only the Lord would be able to get me through the year. I took my hymn book and Bible and went next door to the children's bedroom and spent the hour in Bible reading and prayer and praise, coming into the Lord's presence each day. That was a good preparation for going into chapel where our teachers took turns bringing devotional messages. This was our opportunity to see the spiritual side of our instructors, as in class they played the role of secular university professors.

Chad and I were both assigned to study and analyze Lakota Sioux, an Indian language of North Dakota. We both had the same Indian language helper, an older man from one of the reservations. I found that I could write down the sounds in my notebook, using the symbols of the International Phonetic Alphabet that we had learned in our first year phonetics class. However, then I was stuck, as the Indian man would not say anymore until I correctly repeated the sentence back to him. Try as I would, I could not pronounce the phrase to his satisfaction. Comparing notes with Chad, I found that he had a different problem. He could repeat everything back to our Sioux man just fine, and they had a great session, but afterwards he realized that his notes were very inadequate. We decided to work together. Chad would carry on a conversation with the Indian while

I wrote everything down. In this manner we were able to both fulfill the requirement.

After a few weeks of study, we were each given a grammar of an indigenous language in a traditional model, probably based on Latin. I received a grammar of an Eskimo language of Alaska, written in the Latin model some twenty years before by a missionary to the arctic. We were to rewrite the grammars using the tagmemic model that we were being taught in class. I sat and looked at that grammar and wondered how I would ever complete the assignment.

The next day after lunch, I was faced with the fact that the children had no clean clothes for the next day. I knew I should be working on my grammar paper during the short break after lunch before the afternoon classes began, but since I had no ideas on how to do the paper anyway, I gathered up all the family's dirty clothes and drove to a Laundromat a short distance away from the university. As I folded the children's clothes with my heart stayed upon the Lord and my mind thinking about the Eskimo grammar, I suddenly saw how to do it. I might almost say that I had a vision of the grammatical structure of the language and how to express it in tagmemics. I came back to the university and wrote it up. My paper received a good grade, and Dr. Longacre wrote a little note saying, "You have a very clear method of expression that reminds me of Dr. Gudshinsky." Dr. Sarah Gudshinsky was the renowned literacy expert of the Summer Institute of Linguistics. She would be coming to Grand Forks later in the summer to lecture to us on the making of primers and other literacy materials. I was looking forward to meeting her, and I considered the comparison a great honor.

The day the papers on the grammar project were returned, I ran into John standing by his mailbox with a woeful look on his face. He showed me his paper. It was written by hand in small, tight letters, very hard to decipher. Across the top was scrawled, "I didn't even bother to read this," and the grade was an 'F.' I was as shocked as John. I looked up to John as a superior linguistic student. His familiarity with several languages as well as his knowledgeable questions and comments in class showed that he was one of the most promising students in the second year course. "Why didn't you type your paper?" I asked him. "I never learned how to type," he answered dejectedly.

One morning in our phonology class, the professor decided to spring a pop quiz. The one question was deceptively simple: What are phonemes? We all did our best, and then we handed in our answers. The next morning for some reason Chad got delayed on his way to class. I sat down in the classroom with the others. The professor got up with our quizzes from the previous day in his hand. He proceeded to give us a good scolding for writing such irrelevant answers to his question. "Of all your papers," he told us, "there was only one correct answer, and it was perfect. It was from Chad Stendal who wrote, 'Phonemes are the building blocks of which language is built.'" The professor started into his lecture of the morning, and then the classroom door opened a little, and Chad tried to take his seat as unobtrusively as possible. When the students saw Chad, they let forth with a round of applause and a cheer. You can imagine Chad's confusion and embarrassment, not having a clue what was happening until the professor presented him with his paper and explanation. "That's because of my background in engineering and construction," remarked Chad.

Our friend, Joy, was very depressed. She was finding the course very difficult. One of her roommates became so discouraged that she wanted to drop out and was just barely convinced to stay in the course. We were all feeling the strain. Sometimes we were up all night preparing papers or studying for tests. One of our neighbors in the dorm who was a first year student kindly loaned us an electric coffee maker for these long nights of study. Since Chad had never learned to type, I also had to type his papers. We looked forward to a break in the routine on weekends when social activities among the missionaries and candidates took place, and on Sundays we attended a small Pentecostal church where the music was delightful.

One morning our two friends, Joy and John, walked into our grammar class together. They were laughing and chatting, and I couldn't help but think what an attractive couple they would make. That night, I earnestly prayed that if the Lord could see that they would make a good team for His work that He would put them together.

The summer was drawing to a close. At last we had only the final exams, final interviews, evaluations and field assignments, and then we would be finished with our training. One beautiful August morning we walked into a large assembly hall to take our final grammar examination. The papers were passed out. I looked at mine in disbelief. It appeared to me to be impossible. Leaving my test on my desk, I ran to the adjoining ladies' rest room. Part of this room consisted of a rest area with wicker chairs and sofa. I fell on my knees by a chair and poured my heart out to the Lord. I told him that I could not do this exam in my own strength and pleaded for Him to fill me with his Spirit and do the exam through me. I finished up in my prayer language.

When I returned to my seat and looked at the exam again, everything was different. I could see the patterns in the languages presented and was one of the first to turn in my paper. I left the hall with a good feeling in my heart. I knew that I had passed. Still I was astonished to find out a few days later that I had gotten 100% on the final exam. Some of the staff commented that no one had ever done that before.

Now we were being called in couple by couple or one by one for our final interview, acceptance or rejection, and field assignment. The single candidates were first. Soon we all received a terrible bit of news by way of the grapevine. Both John and Joy had been rejected as missionary candidates. The evaluating committee said that it didn't matter how good John's linguistic ability was if he couldn't communicate his findings on paper because of his poor handwriting and lack of typing skills. Joy was rejected because they thought she would be too much of an emotional drag on any single woman she was teamed with as a partner. I remembered my prayer of a few weeks before, that John and Joy could be a couple. I ran to my room and took out paper and pen. I wrote a letter to the evaluating committee. I explained how Chad and I had to work together as a team, that neither one of us could do the work without the other. I mentioned all John's strong points, what an inspiration he had been to me in the early weeks of first year linguistics. I told about Joy at Jungle Camp, how she had poured her precious cool drinking water on her friend's burned hand and how she had taken the loss of her watch in such a good spirit. I asked that they reconsider John and Joy as a couple and give them another chance.

I was taking a big risk, because at this point, I didn't have a clue as to the relationship between the two of them. All I had to go on was their obvious enjoyment of one another's company that day as they came into class together. To their great surprise John and Joy were called back before the committee and told that if they reapplied as a couple, there was a good chance they could be accepted.

Talking with Joy later, I found out that they were in love, but both had promised the Lord to stay single in order to serve Him better. They had laid their relationship on the altar, and asked Him to make it very clear whether they could serve Him better single or married. They reapplied, married, and the last I knew, they were translating for an Indian tribe in southwest U.S.A.

When the couples were interviewed, we were accepted for service in Colombia, as was the Walton family. Later we were told that because of the critical situation in Colombia, only the best linguists were being sent to Colombia. I'm sure I needed that good final exam in order to qualify.

After a final orientation meeting for all of us who were now ready to go to the foreign field, we took another swing through North and South Dakota, visiting the Meyers and my relatives, and then returned to my parent's home in Minneapolis.

Chapter 15

ℑhe Hand is On the Plow

Minneapolis, Minnesota
Fall 1963

We were now assigned to Colombia and by faith set a departure date of January 3, 1964. We started disposing of our personal belongings and packing the things we would take with us to Colombia. We sold my sterling silver and crystal goblets to help pay our airfare to Colombia. The children emptied their savings accounts for the same purpose. We were asked to speak at a number of churches and other groups presenting our slides of Jungle Camp and telling of our call to Colombia. The children sang songs in Spanish and in *Tzeltal*.

We were attending Bethany Missionary Church. This was an extremely missions minded group who had the goal of having 100 missionaries on the foreign field. Since we were comparatively new members and had not gone through their missionary training program, we did not expect financial support from them. One Sunday evening after the service, Russell and Chad stood in the back of the church looking at a large world map on which small lights indicated the location of the missionaries supported by Bethany. The pastor came over and put his hand on Chad's shoulder. "We will soon be putting up a light for you folks in Colombia," he said. He went on to tell us that the church was planning a commissioning service for us and that we would be receiving a modest amount of monthly support.

As I thought of giving my testimony at our commissioning service, I realized I was caught in a dilemma. I wanted to be honest in my testimony before the membership of Bethany and the ladies of the prayer group, however I was afraid that the presence of my father in the audience would seal my tongue. I had not been able to communicate honestly with my father since our first interest in missions. Any attempt to bring up the subject triggered his lecture on the theory that foreign missions is for a future dispensation, and I knew that I could never shout him down in a argument, or convince him by logic. We were experiencing a calm and were able to live side by side in the same house in peace, and I didn't want to rock the boat. Dad busied himself making beautiful wooden boxes in which to ship our books to Colombia, and he painstakingly stenciled our name and address on all our barrels. Once he even implied that it might be of some value to do Bible translation in this dispensation, as then it would be ready when the Jews went out to evangelize the world. I was fearful of saying something in the commissioning service

that would provoke his wrath and make the rest of our time in Minneapolis miserable.

When the children understood that at the commissioning service the elders would be laying hands on Chad and me and especially commissioning us for the work in Colombia, they asked if they could pass forward to the altar and be prayed for also. They sat in the second row of seats with my parents while Chad and I gave our testimonies. I had prayed much about my testimony, and when my turn came I remember saying that all my life I had always depended on my father in case of emergency. No matter what had gone wrong, or what had broken down, a phone call to him had always brought help. Now that I was going to Colombia beyond his help, God had shown me that He would fill this place in my life. He would always be there when I needed Him.

The pastor told us to kneel at the altar. Chad and I came down from the platform, and the children passed forward. As Sharon moved out into the aisle of the church behind her brothers, she suddenly stopped short. Something was preventing her from going any farther. Puzzled, she stood there struggling against the impediment until Grandpa Dick came to the rescue. The end of the large blue sash on the back of her dress had caught on one of the pews. Grandpa released the sash, re-tied the bow, and Sharon joined the rest of us at the altar. The pastors and the elders commissioned us all to the work in Colombia, and they ordained Chad to the ministry.

As soon as possible after the service, I asked Chad if anything I had said could have possibly offended my father. "I don't see how it could have," he replied, "You compared him to God."

Just before Christmas we went with the Walton family to Rochester, Minnesota to pick up our visas at the Colombian consulate. Sharon was not well, but we took her anyway. By the time we got back to Minneapolis, she was very sick. The doctor prescribed an antibiotic, thinking it was an infection of the urinary tract. She got worse and worse. She had extreme chills and fever. Her temperature went to 106 degrees several times. I mentioned malaria to the doctor, but he stuck with his original diagnosis. In desperation we called for the pastors of Bethany who came right out and anointed her with oil and prayed for her. From that time on, she started to get better.

Right after Christmas, we started for Miami by road. We would sell the car in Miami to help pay the rest of the transportation expenses. We drove through the southern states just ahead of a severe and unusual blizzard. Highways were being closed, and cars were sliding into ditches from the slippery pavement on both sides of us, but we from Minnesota were undaunted. We made it through to Miami just ahead of all the highway closures.

Chapter 16

Welcome to Colombia

January 3, 1964

We met the Walton family in Miami, and after selling our car to some returning missionaries, we boarded a DC-6 of the Pan-American Airline a little after midnight for a six-hour night flight to Bogotá, the capital city of Colombia. As we winged our way south over the ocean, the flight attendants brought us a snack, and at 2 a.m. the children were still wide-awake and full of life. Russell's eyes were sparkling as we flew along over the black waters of the Caribbean. He turned to his father, who was sitting next to him. "We're really having fun, aren't we, Dad?" he remarked.

But Chad was tired. His mind was filled with troublesome thoughts. Would they charge us duty on all our baggage? What problems would we face with our family in this new land? We were going out completely by faith. Our only promised financial support was that mentioned by the pastor at Bethany, and the prospect of Majel Myer's cattle program in the future. At last he turned it all over to the Lord and went to sleep.

At Panama City we all had to get out of the airplane and wait until the fog cleared from *El Dorado*, the International Airport at Bogotá. Accustomed as we were to the frigid temperatures of January in Minnesota, the tropical humidity of Panama City, even at six in the morning, seemed unbearable. By the time we were allowed to board the plane again, I was convinced that I would never be able to stand life in an equatorial clime. As we flew over the Andes Mountains, Chad looked down on the little brown trails winding over the green slopes leading to scattered huts perched on lofty ridges or nestled in little valleys. Later he wrote to my father:

> *Forgotten people—how long have they lived in ignorance, disease, and fear? God is not willing that any should perish. He has not given these people over to sin forever. He has committed to us the ministry of reconciliation.*

As Chad studied the scene below him, I was gazing at our fellow passengers. We had been given a book on Latin American customs as a part of our preparation for Colombia, and from this book, I had been led to believe that Colombians, especially in Bogotá, were very conservative in dress, preferring black and navy blue to any other colors. Chad and Jim Walton had both purchased black topcoats and black hats. I was dressed in a black wool suit with hat and gloves, and Jan too was very conservatively dressed. I noticed that our plane was full of young women beautifully attired in the latest colorful fashion. Their hair was elaborately styled, and their make-up was applied with a lavish hand. "I am certainly going to look like a 'back-number' (an out of style person), if this is how all the people in Bogotá look," I thought.

As the plane started to descend over *El Dorado,* I tried in vain to get into the lavatory to brush my hair and freshen up a bit. Long lines of glamorous ladies stood before all the restroom doors, many repairing their make-up in the aisles. I certainly hadn't been prepared to encounter this preoccupation with personal appearance on the part of the natives of Colombia. I finally gave up trying to get into a restroom and wearily gathered up our hand baggage and our three sleepy, disheveled children to alight from the plane. The Walton family had already descended. As I reached the end of the stairway leading from the plane, cameras flashed, and some young ladies came forward with a beautiful spray of flowers. "Oh my," I thought. "Someone important is being met with flowers and pictures, and here we are, right in the way." I tried to hustle the children off to one side to clear the way for the important arrival, but the girls came right up to us.

"Welcome to the Colombian Branch!" they cried, thrusting the flowers into my arms. I was overwhelmed! All those beautiful women on board that plane, and the flowers were for me.

A few minutes later over a complimentary cup of strong Colombian coffee, the assistant director remarked, "I'll bet it was kind of interesting to be on the flight with all the Miss Universe candidates and their companions."

Aeropuerto El Dorado - Bogotá, Colombia

Chapter 17

A Big Surprise

Bogotá
  January, 1964

To Chad's great relief, we passed through customs without incident and were soon driving towards the city of Bogotá. The city was situated at the eastern edge of a high plateau at 8,600 feet above sea level. This plateau stretched for some 60 miles between the eastern *cordillera* (range) of the Andes and the valley of the Magdalena River. The city from its founding in 1539 had developed in a north-south dimension, lying long and comparatively narrow at the base of the mountains. The highest downtown skyscrapers were dwarfed by the towering peaks of Monserrate and Guadalupe, which rose to the east, some 2,000 feet above the city.

The airport lay to the west of the city, and we now raced towards the mountains in the director's small red Volkswagen, dodging milk cows, pedestrians, and venders of vegetables and cigarettes. We were amazed to see ramshackle huts of scrap lumber, cardboard cartons, and flattened tin cans in corners of vacant lots between modern dwellings. The director explained that due to political unrest in some outlying areas of the country, many had come to Bogotá as refugees from violence and now lived in these makeshift dwellings until they could reorganize their lives.

Soon we pulled up to the Wycliffe group house, the same six-unit apartment building that I had read about in the newsletter while we still lived in Bloomington, Minnesota. We were assigned two adjoining bedrooms on the third floor. Meals would be served in a common dining room, and we had several weeks to get settled and acclimated and ready for an intensive course of Spanish study.

One of the first surprises to me was the chilliness of Bogotá. At this altitude, even its proximity to the equator did not do much to warm up this city with its unheated cement buildings. Even though we had arrived in the dry season, the warmest part of the year, the temperature was usually less than 60 degrees F., and though we had left Minnesota in −20 degree temperatures, Bogotá left us chilled to the bone. We wore our warmest clothes and slept under many blankets.

We were advised to take life easy for the first week or so because of the high altitude. Our fellow missionaries were very friendly and did their best to make us feel welcome. The earliest arrivals had come in late 1962. Some had transferred from other Wycliffe branches, and others had studied Spanish in 1963 and were now out in the tribes. We were a part of twelve, the largest group so far, who would be arriving to participate in the Spanish class that was to start the first of February.

Our apartment was upstairs with a friendly, outgoing couple named Sjaan and John. They had a one-year-old son and were expecting another. Sjaan woke up each morning with nausea and shared all her feelings with me. She had discovered a nice little hospital run by the Worldwide Evangelization Crusade, (WEC), a mission that was well known at Bethany. The prices were reasonable, and Sjaan was well satisfied with the medical care offered by the staff.

Chad and the children were suffering no ill effects from the altitude, but I did not feel well. The other missionaries assured me that for some people the adjustment was difficult, but no one else was having the problems that I was. Our days were filled with orientation lectures and excursions to the historical and cultural attractions of the city, but sometimes I did not feel well enough to go with the group. I wondered how I would ever endure the rigorous pace of Spanish study. Sjaan had some pills that had been prescribed by the doctor for her morning sickness, but she insisted that they were useless. One evening at bedtime, I asked her for one of her pills, and the next morning I woke up feeling fine. "You're going with me when I visit the doctor next week," she declared when I told her.

On the appointed day, we took a taxi forty-two blocks south, parallel to the mountains. It seemed as though the driver who first sounded his horn at an intersection had the right of way, and pedestrians crossed the street at all angles, dodging in and out through the lanes of traffic. We learned that in spite of the bizarre driving customs, accidents were rare. At last we arrived at the center of the city, a place called *tres esquinas* (three corners), where the WEC mission had their headquarters, their largest church, and a small private hospital and outpatient clinic. Sjaan introduced me

to Marion Price, the efficient Australian nurse in charge of the clinic, and Annie Noble, an elderly nurse from Scotland who was the head of the maternity section. Miss Annie's friendly competent manner, and gray hair, done up in a bun, reminded me of my mother.

After tea, served in the manner of the United Kingdom, we were told that the doctor had arrived, and Annie escorted us from the nurses' dining room to the outpatient area of the clinic. I noticed that we were being taken in first, ahead of all the women who had been waiting for an hour or more. This situation embarrassed me, and I demurred, but Miss Annie insisted that it was necessary because she would have to translate for us, and she needed to get back to the delivery room as quickly as possible. I was taken into the examining room first, while Sjaan sat on one of the chairs with the other pregnant women. She occupied herself guessing the ethnic backgrounds represented. The facial features of many revealed the presence of Indian ancestors. Colombian society, we would learn, was composed of at least seven layers of social classes. The clinic served the strata between the lowest and middle levels of the city, roughly the same classes of people as found in the evangelical churches. Here in *La Clínica Emanuel* quality medical care could be obtained for a reasonable price, but the service was not gratis, and thus out of range for the poorest of the poor. Girls from the

WEC churches who had several years of Bible school study were being trained as nurses.

A young nurse, one of the more advanced students, took me into the examining room while Miss Annie went to accompany the doctor on his rounds of the maternity floor. The nurse said something to me in Spanish and with her hand indicated a chair. I sat down on the chair, but that wasn't what she wanted. I tried standing on the scale, but that wasn't right either. I finally understood that I was supposed to take off my dress and place it on the chair. I did so and was looking for a hospital gown or something to put on and saw a white garment hanging on the edge of a folding screen. I took it down and was just going to put it on, when I noticed the doctor's name written inside the collar. It was the doctor's lab coat.

The nurse had gone out, and I had just hung up the lab coat again, when the door opened, and the doctor came in and said something in Spanish. *"No español,"* I called out from behind the screen. The doctor went out to look for Annie, and the young nurse came in again with my medical record card in her hand and tried to pronounce my name.

'I'm here," I called out in English, still hiding behind the screen in my slip.

The nurse had me situated on the examining table by the time the doctor was back with Miss Annie. He thought that I was pregnant but ordered a lab test to make sure. He asked me through Miss Annie how I was going to manage to have my baby in their clinic without knowing Spanish. I replied, again through my interpreter, that I planned to be able to speak Spanish by the time my baby was born. He didn't seem to be much impressed by my optimism and went out shaking his head. *"No español! No español!"* he kept chuckling under his breath.

I kept myself together until we got back to the group house, but then my world fell apart. When I had agreed to come to Colombia to work with primitive Indians, I had not bargained on a pregnancy. The care of a small child had always been a strain on me, and I couldn't imagine handling a new baby under Jungle Camp conditions.

All twelve of the Spanish students had arrived from the USA by now, and the director had called an orientation meeting of all of us together that morning although Sjaan and I had had to miss the first part. Now I took advantage of the solitude of my bedroom to cast myself face down on the double bed for a good cry. At last I arose, wiped my eyes, and washed my face, and decided to go to the meeting. I planned to keep this disconcerting news a secret from everyone except Chad. Back in Minnesota among my relatives and circle of friends, it was the custom to keep a pregnancy secret as long as possible. "It makes the time seem shorter that way," my mother had always said.

I arrived at the room where the meeting was in session and tried to enter as unobtrusively as possible, but as soon as I opened the door, a cheer went up, and amidst hand clapping and congratulations, I was ushered to a chair. Sjaan had gone directly to the meeting and had made the announcement to everyone. It had never occurred to her that I might not want everyone to know yet. The secret was out!

Later that night, Chad and I had a long serious talk in the room that we shared with five-year-old Sharon. We couldn't imagine how this unexpected development had occurred. The next afternoon we took the children for a walk through the middle class residential section of Bogotá where the group house was located. It was a rare warm, sunny day, although a hint of crispness remained in the thin mountain air. The children enjoyed running ahead and balancing on top of waist-high brick or cement walls that separated small grassy plots from the sidewalk in front of many of the buildings. Suddenly Sharon left her brothers and dropped back to walk with Chad and me. "I know how this happened," she told us in a confidential tone. "I have been praying for a baby sister."

Chapter 18

Settling In

All was ready for Spanish study. We had moved downstairs with the Wheeler family, leaving our two bedrooms on the third floor for two young couples that had recently arrived, each with a baby. The Wheelers, a family with four boys, the oldest just younger than Chaddy, had the distinction of being the first Wycliffe people to enter Colombia. They had been working on the Ecuador border with the Siona tribe, and when the contract was signed with Colombia, they had crossed the river, even moving their house to the other side. Al, as an experienced tribal missionary-linguist, was conducting linguistic surveys in the southeastern jungles of Colombia. He was locating likely spots for placing the six linguistic teams that would be available when our class finished Spanish study. Peggy, a devoted mother and registered nurse, was delighted that her boys should have this opportunity to mingle with other North American children for a few months before they returned to their isolated tribal home.

Shortly after moving down with the Wheelers, Sharon became ill again. Her symptoms were the same as those she had experienced in Minnesota, shaking chills followed by high fever. Peggy immediately recognized the disease to be malaria, which Sharon must have picked up in Jungle Camp. After a few days of treatment by "Aunt Peggy," Sharon was fit as a fiddle again.

Chad and I were concerned not only about our children's education, but also how we were going to attend our University classes, leaving them in the care of others for four hours each morning. Peggy offered to help out until such time as her family would leave for their tribal area, but I was loath to leave her with so many children, especially as she was home schooling her oldest son, and it seemed that she had her hands full already. The couples with small children were hiring a Colombian girl to baby-sit their children, but I knew that would never work for my active boys.

Chaddy and Russell were feeling very cooped up in the small apartment with its postage-stamp sized yard in back, so I was taking the risk of letting them play out in the street with the Colombian neighbor children in spite of the fact that some of the Wycliffe people were afraid they might be kidnapped. One day Chaddy brought a friend into the apartment. He was a nicely dressed boy from one of the neighboring apartment buildings. The boys were able to play together all morning, although Chaddy only knew two words in Spanish: *venga* (come) and *mire* (look).

The Christian school in Minneapolis had given me their lessons for the rest of the school year. Russell was in third grade, and Chaddy was in first. I was working with them in these weeks of free time before Spanish classes started, and Russell was making good progress, but I was having trouble with Chaddy. He wanted to look at the pictures in the primer and invent a story about it instead of reading the words printed on the page. While appreciating his creativity, I despaired of ever teaching him to read.

The only other school-aged children in the branch so far were the Townsends, the children of 'Uncle Cam,' the founder of Wycliffe. Elaine Townsend was able to solve the problem of my boys' care during our Spanish study. We registered them in the *Colegio Americano* along with her children. This was a private school run by the Presbyterian Church, the first Protestant mission in Colombia. This was a very elite school and provided the entrance for the Presbyterians into Colombia. They in turn vouched for other missionary groups, such as the WEC. Many Colombian Presidents received their educational start at the Colegio Americano.

The boys were each in a room with 42 boys. Russell made a friend right away who spoke some English, so that was a help to him. Chaddy fit into school very well. He was able to excel in athletics, winning all the races. When I asked him if he had a special friend, he said that all 42 were his special friends. After the first few days, he had added *muy bien* (very good) to his Spanish vocabulary, so I assumed he had been doing all right.

Our Spanish classes were held at the University of the Andes. The campus was built right up the side of the mountain, which required a long uphill climb before we reached the unheated cement classroom buildings. The classrooms were even colder than the group house. Situated as it was in the shadow of the mountain, the rays of the sun never even reached the outside walls. The method taught was strictly auditory and conversational. I learn best visually and was lost after the first day.

Somehow some of the correspondence sent us by the branch while we were in Minneapolis had gone astray, and we had never been informed of the cost of the Spanish course, but Chad was able to work in the engineering department of the University in return for our tuition.

We discovered a kindergarten just a few blocks from the group house, and since it was called *Kinder en Ingles* (Kindergarten in English) we decided that it would be just the place for Sharon and two other little girls near her age. We didn't know that although a show was made of using English materials, the teachers did not know how to pronounce English. After a few days Sharon came home shaking her head. "I don't know what language they use in my kindergarten," she told us. "It isn't English, and it isn't Spanish.

After awhile the girls came home with a new Spanish word, *necio,* that according to our director's wife meant naughty and perhaps a little stupid. It seemed that they were not doing so well.

Meanwhile, Sjaan and I felt that we had found the perfect garments to wear to school. The tourist shops were selling Colombian *ruanas,* woolen wrap-around ponchos that were ample and warm and came in many different colors. We found the *ruanas* to be just the thing to keep us warm and hide our growing abdomens. One day we were scolded by a woman professor who was wearing a trim, tailor-made wool suit. "Don't you know that *ruanas* are only worn by the poor, the sick, and North Americans?"

"I qualify on all counts," I responded.

As the weeks wore on Russell didn't seem to be very happy at school. At first he had been enthusiastic, but soon he was trying to find excuses to stay at home. After being questioned by Chad, he revealed that he was upset because he couldn't understand what the teacher said to him. Chad went right out and bought him a Spanish-English dictionary and showed him how to look up words. Russell took the dictionary and went back to school again.

It came time for me to pay the tuition for the boys' studies. Peggy Wheeler taught me to say, *Quiero pagar por mis hijos.* "(I want to pay on behalf of my sons.) *Pagar* is the Spanish word for 'pay.' The 'a' has the sound of 'ah' as in 'father.'

All the way to the school, I kept repeating, *Quiero pagar por mis hijos, Quiero pagar por mis hijos,* but by the time I arrived, the sound of 'ah' had changed to 'ay' as in the English word, pay. I walked up to the girl at the desk and said, *"Quiero pegar por mis hijos."* The Spanish word, *pegar*, means 'hit,' so I had said, "I want to hit on behalf of my sons." The girl looked up startled, as if she expected me to punch her in the nose. But seeing my North American face and the money in my hand, she smiled.

"Pagar, pagar," she corrected me, accepting my money and giving me a receipt.

A few days later, Russell came home from school at noon very distraught. The teacher had taken his dictionary away from him and called the principal. I must return with him in the afternoon to the principal's office. The principal was an understanding North American woman. She told me that the teacher was very incensed at Russell because he would not obey her. I explained that Russell did not understand Spanish. She said that the teacher refused to believe that. The teacher was convinced that Russell understood Spanish well and was simply disobedient. At last the teacher was called in. The principal once again told the teacher that Russell did not understand Spanish. The teacher said that she could not believe that because when his turn came to read, Russell could read perfectly.

Since Spanish has a very phonetic alphabet, Chad had taught Russell the sounds of all the Spanish vowels and consonants. He could stand up and read so that the others could understand him, but he did not understand it himself. The principal understood the problem at once, but the teacher was dubious. An uneasy truce was declared, and Russell went back to the classroom.

Chapter 19

The Llanos

The Llanos, March 1964

While we were occupied with Spanish study, Al Wheeler was doing tribal surveys, and our director, Clarence Church, was looking for the right spot to build a "base," a center for the linguistic and translation work in Colombia. Since most of the known tribal groups were located in the southeastern jungles and eastern plains of the country, he had decided that a spot out in the *Llanos Orientales* (eastern plains) of Colombia would be ideal. It would be far enough out so that the land was not too valuable, but close enough to Bogotá so that it could be supplied by road. In addition, since most of the tribes in Peru and Ecuador were served by float planes, and since it was assumed that it would be the same in Colombia, a large body of water long enough to land a plane on floats would be a must.

An airplane and pilot loaned to us from the Peru branch helped our director look for the ideal location. One evening in late February, the director called us all together and told us that a site had been found. He and the pilot had actually landed on a flat area of grassland near a large lake. A friendly farmer had driven them around on his tractor, and they were convinced that the property near the lake would make an ideal location for the translation center.

Later we met the "friendly farmer." His name was Emiliano Parra. He owned a cattle farm right across the road from the small improvised airstrip on which they had landed. He and his family had come to know the Lord through listening to a Christian radio station out of the Netherlands Antilles, called Bonaire. He was so delighted with this radio station that he renamed his farm Bonaire. Emiliano and his son Rafico became faithful friends of the Wycliffe Bible Translators, and personal friends of the Stendal family.

Chad and a companion were asked to go to the site over a long weekend in early March and survey the area with a transit Chad borrowed from the engineering department at the University of the Andes. They traveled by bus on the winding mountain road that led up and over the mountain pass at some 10,000 feet above sea level, then meandered through the mountains for several hours before descending to the sweeping grasslands of the eastern plains. After passing through the small city of Villavicencio, better known as Villavo, the capital of the department of Meta, the road straightened out and continued on to the ancient town of San Martin.

San Martin was first founded in 1536 by the German conqueror, Nicolás de Federman. A group of Spanish and German explorers had landed on the shores of Venezuela soon after 1525 and trekked overland seeking gold. Their privations and sufferings were tremendous, but were nothing compared to the suffering they inflicted on the native people and cultures in their paths. A trade existed among the various tribes exchanging salt for gold. The Indians as far away as the coast possessed golden objects, but the explorers wanted to find the source of the gold, the gold mines. They had been told that the trail of salt would lead to *El Dorado* (the Golden One) the source of the gold. By the time the weary explorers followed the trail of salt to the site of the future San Martin, they had been reduced to eating their horses that had died of exhaustion and boiling their leather bootlaces for nourishment. Their metal tools and hardware had worn out, and they had replaced them with the gold they had wrested from the Indians, the only metal in the area. They founded the ancestor village of San Martin while recuperating their strength to continue searching for a pass through the Andes. Finally the pass was discovered, and they were one of the three groups of Europeans to converge on the plateau of Bogotá, in 1539. Thus San Martin is older than Bogotá.

Later, the village was refounded by the Spanish captain, Pedro Daza, in 1585. This town, called *Medina de Las Torres*, was burned down by the local Indians and rebuilt in 1641 and renamed, *San Martin de Tours*, commemorating St. Martin of Tours of AD 397, who as a young soldier of only 15 years is renowned for giving half of his cloke to a shivering man on a cold winter day. The town is much older than the surrounding villages and is controlled by families who trace their lineage back for many generations. San Martin today is a center of *llanero* folklore. Tourists come from near and far in November each year to celebrate a special festival that includes the famous Quadrilles of San Martin. This spectacular performance of horses and riders that commemorates the struggles between Arabs and Spanish in Spain, and the struggles between the Indians and Spanish, aided by their black slaves, in the New World. The honor of participating in these quadrilles is hereditary, passing from generation to generation, father to son.

This town became important in Stendal family history as well. Years later, it would be our home. San Martin was the end of the line for regular bus service in 1964, but transportation from this point was provided by the colorful *chivas* (literally, nanny goats). The name probably had something to do with the roughness of the ride. These vehicles consisted of brightly colored wooden frames built over old trucks. The *chivas* contained wooden benches for passengers, but there were no springs and no hand brakes. A boy about ten with a brick in each hand rode in the back of the *chivas* and if the vehicle stalled on an upgrade, he jumped out and placed a brick behind each back tire. There was no regular road, just tracks through the *Llanos* and each vehicle sought its own route. From the air these vehicle tracks looked like braided ropes with many tracks crisscrossing each other but all going to the same destination. Chad and his friend finally arrived at the designated area, surveyed a square kilometer, placed four concrete posts to mark the corners, and returned to Bogotá the way they had come.

Chapter 20

The Long Wait

The weeks of Spanish study dragged on. I did not feel like I was making much progress in the Spanish language. I didn't have much time to study as I was teaching the children their English lessons in the afternoons. Since I learn best visually, I really missed having a book. Books were available to be purchased in the USA, we were told. Occasionally one of our fellow students would loan me a book for an afternoon.

I longed to communicate with the employees in the group house. A formidable cook named Lucila ruled the kitchen. She was assisted by Ana and Sara, sisters whose father was a pastor. They were reported to have come to Bogotá as refugees from the violence in outlying parts of the country. Looking back I wonder if they had been traumatized by their experiences. They went about their work in an absorbed way and did not seem open to friendly overtures. Another woman, Señora Rosa, was employed to handle the group laundry. She spent afternoons ironing and seemed more approachable for small talk. I put together simple sentences and tried to communicate with her. Often I could not understand her responses, but I tried to look intelligent even though I couldn't completely understand what she was saying. I would nod my head and say, "*Si* (yes)." I thought I was doing quite well, until one day I overheard her say to Ana, "That *Señora* Patricia doesn't understand anything. She just says, *Si,* all the time."

However Chad made a bigger blunder in his use of the Spanish language. One Saturday morning, the announcement was made that Lucila needed the helping hand of a man in the kitchen, and Chad was assigned the duty. At the appointed time, Chad appeared in the kitchen and announced to this middle-aged single lady, "Yo soy su hombre. (I'm your man.) He made the mistake of using the verb *soy* (a permanent state), instead of *estoy* (a temporary state). That was too much for dignified, sober Lucila, and she almost split her sides with laughter. After that, she always had a special place in her heart for Chad.

Uncle Cam Townsend, the founder of Wycliffe, and his wife, Elaine, were making their home in Bogotá. Uncle Cam had previously been the acting director, and his presence was deemed necessary in this very delicate diplomatic situation between Wycliffe and the Colombian government. While we were in Spanish study, Uncle Cam and Elaine left on a survey trip to Russia to investigate the possibility of Bible translation in the numerous indigenous languages in the Soviet Union. They asked us to take care of their ten-year-old son, Billy. Naturally, Billy was somewhat saddened by the absence of his parents, so at Easter time, Chad bought three baby ducks, one for each of the boys. He surmised correctly that this would cheer up Billy and give the boys something to do in the cooped up Group House. The ducks lived in the bathroom of one of the six apartments. Periodically the boys plugged up the shower drain so the ducks could have a swim. Since this apartment was unoccupied, the tremendous mess that the ducks made on the tile floor of the bathroom didn't matter very much. However after a few weeks, several young couples came in from their tribal assignments and were given bedrooms in that apartment and used that bathroom. I thought they were very good-natured about sharing the bathroom with the ducks. I was extremely embarrassed about the situation, but I didn't know what to do about it. Carpeted bathrooms were a new decorating trend in the United States in those days. One day two of the young women were scanning a home decorating magazine. I came by just in time to hear one of them say, "Don't you think what Pat needs is a bathroom like this?" She was pointing to a picture of a lovely designer bathroom with white carpeting. I am sure they were imagining what a mess those ducks would make of a white carpeted bathroom. We found that in general these young people who had just spent months in a primitive tribe with marginal living conditions were very happy and thankful for the comforts of the Bogotá apartment. They brought a lot of life to our Wednesday night prayer meetings as they gave us fresh, specific requests. On Sunday evenings we all gathered to hear a tribal report from one of the recently returned missionaries.

While we were in Spanish study, we attended several information sessions in which Al Wheeler oriented us as to the results of the surveys he had undertaken. I believe all of these surveys were to the southeastern part of Colombia where many small jungle tribes lived. There were a number of small tribes all belonging to the Tucano family. These languages were related to one another, and since a man must marry a woman from a language group different from his own, all of these people knew several languages. Al also identified small tribes that were completely unrelated to the dominant group. Among the latter were two of the slave tribes that had so touched our hearts in Jungle Camp. As Chad and I listened to the reports, we expected that the Lord would lay his finger on one of these tribes for us. The Waltons felt called to go to a small tribe in the Amazon Basin where they have done a wonderful work. Others answered the call to other tribes. We had such a definite call to the mission field and to Colombia that we wanted to be sure that we did not miss the call of God to the special tribe where He wanted us to work. However we did not seem to hear that inner voice from the Lord saying, "This is the tribe where I want you."

Finally June came, and Spanish study was over. Five men, including Chad, and one woman with her baby, were sent out to start construction on our new base. It was named Lomalinda (beautiful hills). The terrain consisted of rolling hills, separated by valleys. These hills were composed of a hard, unfertile substance and only supported scanty plant life; however, the black soil in the valleys gave root to palm trees and other jungle vegetation. Parrots and colorful birds of all kinds made their homes in the trees. The taller palms down by the lake were home to various kinds of monkeys, including large red howler monkeys. Several kinds of alligators lived in small rivers at the inlet and the outlet of the lake, and according to the locals, a monster lived in the lake itself along with piranha, other fish, and various kinds of snakes, especially anacondas (water boas). That probably accounted for the fact that the country people built their few houses far away from the lake, leaving plenty of room for the strange *gringos* (originally in Mexico, a derogatory name for Americans, but we accepted it in good humor). They were curious to see what the monster would do to us.

A large loma (hill) near the lake with a broad level expanse on top was designated Loma 1, and the first construction took place in that area. The plan was to build six one-room "temporary" buildings around a central wash house. A large permanent dining hall/kitchen was to be constructed off to one side. This would also serve as our assembly hall and church for many years to come. Until the buildings were up, the missionaries would live Jungle Camp style in jungle hammocks slung from the palm trees. Jerri Morgan, the one woman who went in the first group, would cook on an apartment-sized gas stove set up under a canvas tarp.

I didn't see this firsthand since it was decided that Sjaan Waller and I, the two pregnant women, should stay in Bogotá until our babies were born. An August due date was set for each of us. The doctor didn't seem too pleased with the way my pregnancy was going. At five months he informed me that my baby would be born breech. I wasn't worried about it, as I was sure the baby would turn several somersault in the four months that were left before the delivery date.

Mother wrote that the ladies in my prayer group were having a shower for me. I waited with great anticipation for the next shipment from Miami to arrive. Finally the day came, and sure enough not one, not two, but three or four boxes were marked with my name. Lo and behold, to my dismay and chagrin, in the boxes were all my old maternity and baby clothes that I had left in Mother's basement to be given away. There they were, the tired old clothes that had seen me through three pregnancies, and the old stained shirts and baby blankets, yellow with age. To be sure, the ladies had sent me a new maternity dress, and a few new baby clothes, and Dorothe, bless her heart, had sent me a complete set of baby bottles with plastic, disposable liners, a new invention. Disposable diapers were still in the future. After my initial shock and disappointment, I soaked all the baby clothes in bleach and removed some of the stains, but the maternity clothes for the most part were a lost cause. I couldn't wear them in classy, stylish Bogotá.

We and the Wallers were living on a minimum of financial support. Sjaan and I decided that we would have to be very frugal in providing clothing for our new arrivals. Sjaan found a place in downtown Bogotá where the poorest people shopped and remnants of cotton yard goods could be bought for a few pesos. Jan Walton loaned me her sewing machine, and I turned out little sleepers, shirts, and wrapping blankets. I even collected scraps from other missionaries and made four quilts, one for each Stendal child, including the anticipated new arrival. All of this sewing somehow helped my mental health and gave me an emotional link with my family roots here in this strange land. My dearly loved Grandma Windburn had made quilts almost right up to her dying day. Somehow, I felt I was doing what I was supposed to do, even though I might end up a monolingual quilt-maker.

Every month, in addition to the money sent by Bethany, we would have a number of gifts of five, ten, or fifteen dollars sent by different people. It fell to me to write the thank-you letters. This was a very difficult task for me. The only way I could accept donations at all, was to accept them as from the Lord. If the Lord moved upon the people to give, I could accept the gift. I was very thankful to the Lord, but it was hard for me to find words to thank the donors. An interesting fact was that apart from Bethany, there were few donors that were on the list every month. One month the additional money that we needed so badly would come from one source, and the next month from another. My heart was touched by the different people who were helping us, but I suffered trying to find words to express my heartfelt thanks. Once in a while we sent a typed letter to Bethany, and they printed it and sent it to the list of some two-hundred names that we had compiled. Chad almost always was the author of these communications. I tried to write good newsy personal letters to key people such as Genie Dean, and my former neighbor, June Meidema, as well as to my parents and sister Dorothe so they could get a feel for the events we were experiencing. It was hard to write to Chad's parents, as they didn't want to know anything about the missionary work, and there wasn't much else to write about.

At that time we had a way of receiving packages from Miami. Although we were asked to keep our requests for stateside items to a minimum, so many people were coming from Miami to Colombia that we could have packages sent to a Miami address where they would be added to the shipment of the next new missionary coming to join us. By May, new couples were already arriving to be a part of the next Spanish course that would start in July. Mother had sent us a care package. I remember it included my electric toaster and a small baking set for Sharon, complete with all the necessary baking utensils and several miniature baking mixes. She would use the apartment oven for her baking.

Since we were all in Spanish study, six days out of the week breakfast was made by Lucila and served by Ana and Sara. None of them had the concept of warm, buttered toast. They toasted the bread, and then when it was cold, they smeared it with cold, softened margarine. I had asked Mother to send my toaster, so we could eat some nice warm buttered toast. The next Sunday after the toaster arrived, Chaddy grabbed the toaster and volunteered to make the toast. He took the toaster to the big group kitchen. It seemed like he was gone a long time, but he finally emerged with a whole loaf of bread toasted and piled up high on a plate. It was totally cold and spread with cold unmelted margarine. "Just like the maids' toast," he proudly announced, and it was.

Chad came from the llanos to visit us after a few weeks. He planned to take Billy and Russell back to Lomalinda with him as soon as the first temporary building was up. While he was with us, a radio message from Lomalinda requested a broom. We all assumed that if a broom was being ordered, the first building must be up. Chad returned to Lomalinda with Billy and Russell, the broom, and a bicycle. He felt that a bicycle was necessary for the missionaries at the base to be able to get to the town of Puerto Lleras in an emergency or to supplement their diet by buying vegetables, eggs, or meat. We could not possibly afford to buy one with our slim income, but he pushed the idea through whatever committee was necessary to release group funds.

I sent the ducks to Lomalinda with Billy and Russell. A few weeks later, Clarence Church, the director came back from Lomalinda in his cute little Volkswagen bug. He told us that no building was roofed yet. The broom had been ordered because the floor had been installed. Billy and Russell were sleeping in jungle hammocks like the other missionaries. However, when Clarence left, Chaddy was happily seated in the red Volkswagen. Chad had given word to bring Chaddy to Lomalinda as well. He knew how hard it was for me to keep him occupied in the Group House. At this point an idyllic existence started for Chaddy and Russell. The one-room cabin designated for the Stendal family was up and roofed. Chad built beds and a table. He gave the boys their school assignments each morning before he went to work. Russell was doing his third grade assignments and was also to help Chaddy with his first grade lessons if necessary. Chad used a carrot and a stick approach. If the assignments were not finished at the end of the day, they got the stick. If the work was completed they each got a piece of hard candy. As Chad tells it, he never had to use the stick, but he ran out of candies.

In addition to school work, helping to carry water from the lake, and washing dishes, the boys had a lot of fun with pet animals, swimming in the lake (in spite of the piranhas) and just running free across the *Llanos*. They made friends with the local people, some of whom had been hired to work at Lomalinda. By the time I saw them again, they were tanned, muscular, and were quite proficient in Spanish.

Soon trucks were being dispatched from Bogotá with building materials for Lomalinda. The loaded trucks made a final stop at the group house before starting out on the 10 to 12 hour trip, winding through the mountains to Villavicencio, and then over the primitive road to Lomalinda. Sjaan and I and the other women whose husbands were out building the new base, baked bread, cookies and other goodies and even canned some meat to send out to Lomalinda on the trucks.

Sharon got very interested in baking. Even though she was only five years old, she learned to follow directions explicitly and clean up her own mess. She soon used up all the mixes that came with her baking set.

Chapter 21

At Last

With all the men in our family gone, Sharon and I moved to a small room with bunk beds. As she watched my abdomen getting larger and larger, she said to me one day, "Mom, I'm really sorry I prayed for this baby. I didn't know about this pregnant business. I just thought you were going to lay an egg."

It seemed that the baby was still in a breech position as the large, hard head was pushing against my lungs. Together with the high altitude of Bogotá, I wasn't getting enough oxygen. Several times I had visual disturbances, and I was ordered to bed for a few days. It was just at that time that Sharon got the strong desire to do more baking with her little baking set. Since there were no more mixes, I had her find my Betty Crocker Cookbook. From my bed I divided the recipes in quarters or eighths so they would fit in her tiny pans. I gave her directions one step at a time from my bed, and she managed to produce tiny cakes and cookies. One time she even made bread. The other ladies were amazed and were especially happy that she left the kitchen as clean or cleaner than she had found it.

As the time drew closer and closer to the birth of the baby, Sharon got more and more agitated. She really didn't want another brother, she confided to me. She would rather not have a baby at all if it were going to be a boy. She prayed ferverently that the baby would be a girl. One morning Sharon woke up all smiles. "I finally figured out what we can do with that baby if it comes, and it is a boy," she announced. "We can send it out to Lomalinda to the men on the first truck leaving."

In early August Chad and the boys, together with John Waller, returned to Bogotá. We all moved back to the same third floor apartment we had shared in the beginning. Chad and I with Sharon had a large, sunny room, originally planned to be the dining room of the apartment. Our boys had a small bedroom in the middle and at the end of the hall by the bathroom, Sjaan and John Waller and little Jonathan had their bedroom. We all went into baby watch mode. I believe it was August 12 that little Steven Waller made his appearance. Sharon was more worried than ever about our baby turning out to be a boy.

Chad accompanied me to the clinic for my weekly check-up. I had been amazed to learn that although the doctor saw me on all my prenatal visits, and would see me after the birth, the actual delivery was attended by Miss Annie or Marian Price, the head of the clinic who was also a nurse-midwife. I had made great friends with Miss Annie. She always invited us up to the nurses' lounge for tea. Miss Annie was always asking if we had decided on our tribe yet. She was from Scotland and was a member of the Worldwide Evangelization Crusade (WEC). Our church, Bethany Fellowship, worked closely with this mission. Miss Annie knew some of the same Christian leaders that we had heard speak at Bethany, so we felt somewhat of a common bond with this little indomitable gray-haired lady.

On this particular morning, as Chad and I sipped our tea with Miss Annie, waiting for the arrival of the doctor, Annie remarked, "If you want to work with Indians, why don't you go to those dirty little people who live in the Sierra Nevada de Santa Marta."

"Who are these dirty, little people?" replied Chad, intrigued.

Annie went on to tell all she knew about them. As a young single missionary girl from Scotland, she had worked at the United Fruit Company in northern Colombia. Her mission had been left without funds during World War II, and she had gone to work as a nurse in order to support a married couple and several other single ladies. On her vacations, she had often gone up into the Sierra Nevada de Santa Marta, the high mountain area on the north coast of Colombia. She went there to escape the oppressive heat of the banana zone and to rest at a mission station, Carmelo, that had been started by some missionaries from Canada. Carmelo had a Bible Institute for Colombian young people and a home and school for the children of English-speaking missionaries. While she was at Carmelo, several Indians had come to pay a visit. Annie was shocked by their very short stature and their seeming disregard for cleanliness. She understood that many of them lived several hours by trail from Carmelo. Chad was very interested in Annie's account of these Indians. Neither our Wycliffe leaders nor the general Colombian public was aware of their existence. Annie offered to set him up with a letter of introduction to the director of Carmelo after our baby was born.

I was having more and more trouble with lack of oxygen. The baby was still in a breech position, and I was ordered to bed rest again. I was having what is known as Braxton-Hicks contractions, painless, but very intense. Annie did not seem to be very familiar with these, and because the baby was breech and I was having these contractions, she decided to hospitalize me. I brought along quilt squares to sew together by hand, and books to read, but Miss Annie would not let me have either one. To her, bed rest was bed rest, with your head on a low pillow, not propped up or sitting in bed. I was soon so bored, I didn't know what to do.

The clinic was in the very heart of Bogotá. This was the WEC headquarters in Colombia. The complex consisted of a church, a print shop, and a Christian bookstore, as well as living quarters for some of the missionaries. The neighborhood had deteriorated. The one thing I could do was look out the window, but all I could see was a long, dingy block wall across the street. This wall seemed to be a favorite place for taxi drivers to stop. The drivers as well as other men who strolled by would do what is referred to in the King James Version of I Samuel 25:22. This made me more depressed than ever. The building behind the wall was just a little bit lower than my hospital room. The roof seemed to be the exercise area for a hospital for elderly demented women. They were all dressed in strange outfits, and one of them frequently did a little dance. Several built a small fire, and warmed some unidentifiable substance that they seemed to enjoy as a picnic snack. The atmosphere was extremely depressing. My heart went out to these unfortunates, but I couldn't think of any way to help them. Watching the dramas unfolding outside my window did nothing to entertain me. When I mentioned the situation to Annie, she solved the problem by pulling down my window shade.

Several times people came in and tried to turn the baby around to a head down position. They were completely unsuccessful. The baby refused to budge. One morning a young nurse stuck her head around the corner of my room and said what I understood as, *"Posicion normal?"* She was making a mark on a checklist attached to a clipboard, and was ready to go on her way, when I shouted, *"No! No es normal!"*

The girl looked very startled and stuck her head back in my room. *"La cabeza está arriba."* (The head is up.) I gravely informed her. I thought she was asking about the baby's position, and I didn't want her to write down 'normal.' I didn't know how to tell her in Spanish that the position of the baby was breech. Actually she was asking a routine question. '*Deposicion*' was a polite way to refer to a bodily function.

Later in the day, a dining room employee asked me if I wanted *agua de panela* or *tetero*. I knew that *agua de panela* was warm brown sugar water. I knew I didn't want that so I thought I would try the other option. I had no idea what it was, but since the missionaries running the clinic were from the United Kingdom I thought it might be tea. At least it started with the right letter of the alphabet. The girl marked down my order, and as she was leaving I added, "*Sin dulce*" (without any sweetening). She looked somewhat startled but left without comment. A little while later Miss Annie bustled into my room. "What in the world did you want?" she asked me sharply. "You have the kitchen in an awful uproar."

"I just wanted a cup of tea without sugar," I replied meekly.

"Well, why didn't you say so in the first place?" Miss Annie demanded. She had been called from the delivery room to find out what the *gringo* lady wanted to drink. Later I found out that *tetero* was warm brown sugar water with milk added. The kitchen was in consternation as to how to bring me unsweetened *tetero*.

The next morning my breakfast tray arrived with no beverage. I finally got a hold of the girl who was serving the breakfast trays to ask where my coffee was. Somehow she was able to make me understand that Miss Annie had given strict orders to the kitchen that I was not to be given anything to drink except unsweetened tea. When they got all the breakfast trays served, they were going to make my tea. After a few days, I was released from the hospital – still with no baby.

August was drawing to a close and the mission was organizing a school; a teacher would arrive soon. Several more families had come with school-aged children. Like an old fire horse smelling smoke, I helped Elaine Townsend organize the school materials. I wished I could volunteer to be one of the teachers myself and forget about Spanish and having babies. Then I experienced another episode of visual disturbances and was sent back to bed again. One of the translators, Isabel Kerr, a dear friend, was drafted as the other teacher. She could not go to the tribe yet because her partner had been delayed. She would be Russell's teacher.

A few days before school was to start, I heard that the teacher for the younger children had arrived. I asked that the new teacher be brought to my bedside. Her name was Kathy and she was a pretty woman in her early twenties with lots of enthusiasm. I tried to explain to her that she would have two of my children in her class, Sharon was in first grade and already knew how to read (she had looked over my shoulder while I was trying to teach Chaddy). As I told her that Chaddy was in second grade but only wanted to look at the pictures, I broke down and cried. "That's okay," Kathy told me. "We will make school so much fun for him this year that he will love it, and next year he will want to learn to read." At least that was how I understood what she said. I was not much comforted. I had visions of Chaddy going into third grade still unable to read.

The first day of school, I woke up with what could be interpreted as real labor pains. I will spare you all the details of the breech delivery. Sufficient to say that Annie had to call for the doctor. About noon, Gloria Anne made her appearance. I didn't get to see Sharon's face when Chad told her about her baby sister, but there was no more talk about sending the baby out to Lomalinda on the truck.

True to her word, Annie Noble wrote the director at Carmelo a letter of introduction. When Gloria turned three weeks old, Chad flew to Santa Marta with a free ticket from Avianca, the Colombian airline. This amazing story is told in detail in his book *High Adventure in Colombia*. Now that Gloria was born safely, our family could begin the work we had come to Colombia to do—or so we thought.

Chapter 22

A Door Opens

Bogotá,
September, 1964

I had my own problems after Chad left for the Sierra Nevada de Santa Marta. I was left on my own with now – four children and one of them a newborn. It seemed like all my teeth had chosen that moment to start aching. I had to get them fixed, because as soon as Chad came back, our whole family was going out to Lomalinda to live in the little cabin he had built. I was sent to a very good dentist who fixed the aching teeth, but what a time I had figuring out what to do with the baby. Once in awhile I could find a babysitter, but I hated to impose on people who also had busy lives. Sometimes I left Gloria in her infant seat on the floor of the dentist's office. Sometimes she screamed the whole time I was in the dentist's chair.

The Waller family was also going out to Lomalinda to live. Their new baby, Steven, was just two weeks older than Gloria. One day Sjaan came to have a serious talk with me. Both of our families were on low income, but John Waller had located a wonderful refrigerator being sold by someone who was leaving Colombia. Sjaan wanted to know if our two families could buy it together. We would be living in neighboring cabins at Lomalinda. Sjaan wanted the refrigerator to be kept in her cabin, and when they could, they would buy out our share. In the meantime, we would have the use of half of it. I agreed to the arrangement. I knew that meat was brought from the nearby town once a week, and we would need some way to keep it from spoiling. I didn't know where the money would come from, but it seemed to be a wonderful opportunity.

Every time I went downstairs for meals, it seemed like someone asked me about Chad. It was becoming very hard to keep saying that I hadn't heard from him. We were going into the red with the extra expenses of the baby and the dental work, and I didn't know what to do about that. On top of everything else, I realized that the baby had a problem. Because of the cold in Bogotá, she was always wrapped up in blankets so no one noticed, but when I bathed her or changed her diaper, I realized that there was something wrong with her left leg. I took her back to see the doctor who had attended her birth, but he examined her foot and said it was just fine. He mildly rebuked me for being an overly anxious mother. I remembered that one of Sharon's feet had turned out at birth, and it had just been a matter of muscular development to bring it into line. Gloria's turned in, so I assumed it was the same sort of problem.

I had expected Chad to be gone about a week, but the time dragged on with no word from him. After three weeks, Russell looked sadly at Gloria and remarked, "Daddy has been gone for half of Gloria's life."

One day I found Sjaan waiting for me with (for her) excellent news. They had received an unexpected gift from home, and now they wouldn't need our help with the purchase of the refrigerator. Somehow that was the last straw. I went to my room and cried like a baby. Now how was I going to keep our meat from spoiling? I was really angry at Chad for going away and leaving me for so long.

In a day or two, the director came to see me. Chad had called the office. He was on his way back to Bogotá and was bringing two Kogi Indians with him. Chad's amazing story has been told in detail in *High Adventure in Colombia*. Suffice it to say here that he had been very miraculously led by the Lord to Santiago Dingula, probably the only Kogi Indian who would have wanted to fly in an airplane and go to Bogotá. (See chapter 12 in *Minnesota Mom Volume I*) The Kogi Indians are extremely reclusive and introverted. They do not want any contact with the outside world. Chad had finally arrived at Santiago's little house deep in the Sierra. At first Santiago refused to admit that the language he spoke was not the same as Spanish, but while Chad was trying to get some Kogi words from him, a large airplane flew overhead. Santiago forgot about Chad and put all his attention on the airplane until it was out of sight. After the airplane was gone, Chad remarked that he had come from Bogotá on an airplane like that. Santiago's response was completely unexpected. "Take me to Bogotá in an airplane, and I will teach you my language." Now they were on their way.

The news that Chad was coming with two Kogi Indians caused quite a stir in the Wycliffe Group House. For one thing, there were no empty rooms available. Our family was sharing an apartment with the Waller family. There was a large living room with what used to be known as a "daybed" instead of a sofa. It was like a bed with a lot of cushions and pillows to put behind your back when you sat on it like a sofa. Some wondered if the Indians could sleep there.

Our apartment was on the third floor, and when Chad made his entrance one evening, quite a few of our missionary friends followed him and the Indians up the stairs to see the look on my face when I opened the door. I admit I was flabbergasted. All the jungle Indians who had come to Bogotá looked pretty much like any other country Colombian. But I had never imagined anything like these two Indians. I didn't even know if they were men, women, or children. Their short height was childlike. Their long hair seemed womanish, but their faces and manner indicated that they had to be men. They were very happy and went straight to the daybed. They snuggled their heads into the pillows, their feet just coming over the edge of the daybed. Santiago announced that they were going to sleep right there. They had never found anything so comfortable.

As the Kogis relaxed on the daybed, they each pulled a big, black cigar out of their *mochilas* (carrying bags) and lit them. Such a vile odor had never before been released into the pure, smoke-free air of our missionary home. The house mother quickly told them in Spanish about our no smoking policy, and the cigars were extinguished.

Before they went to sleep, Chad took the Kogis into the bathroom and showed them how to use everything. In the middle of the night we were awakened by the sound of water running. Chad got up to find the two Kogis in the bathroom turning on all the faucets and repeatedly flushing the toilet while peering underneath, trying to find out where all the water was going.

The next morning I had a better look at the Indians. Santiago had a wizened brown face with an amazing number of horizontal wrinkles in his forehead. He was enjoying himself immensely. He was friendly and talkative, like one whose fondest fantasies have just come true. His companion, Wenceslao, on the other hand was timid and fearful. Half of his face was a mottled color of red and purple, the result of a mosquito-borne disease known medically as "pinta." We discovered that this disease could be cured by three shots of long-acting penicillin administered one each month. We started him on his first shot of the treatment, and eventually all the disfiguration disappeared.

Uncle Cam Townsend, the founder of Wycliffe, was living in one of the apartments with his wife, Elaine, and his two youngest children, just a little older than ours. Uncle Cam was delighted with the visitors. He arranged an appointment for them with the Colombian Minister of Government and other important personages in downtown Bogotá. Just before they left the apartment to keep the appointments, Chad asked the Kogis if they wanted to use the bathroom. At that point I disappeared down to second floor to visit with some of my friends. I felt the need for debriefing after the events of the last 12 hours. Gloria was napping, the other children were in school, and I was confident that Chad and our visitors were downtown seeing the important officials.

Later when I returned to our apartment, what a sight met my eyes! Elaine Townsend and Chad were each trying to dry out a very damp Indian with a hair dryer. When Chad had asked them if they wanted to use the bathroom, they used everything, including the shower, fully dressed. Their long black hair was completely drenched. The Indians sat there sheepishly, wondering what they did wrong.

"Patty, where were you?" Chad shouted above the noise of the two hair dryers. They had looked high and low for me, but I couldn't be found, so Elaine had come to the rescue to help Chad dry out the Indians. Uncle Cam was on the phone, rescheduling the appointments for later in the day. At last the Kogis were pronounced dry enough to go outside. Chad certainly didn't want them to come down with pneumonia or anything else on their visit to civilization. Most primitive Indians are very vulnerable to white man's diseases; however the Kogis did not seem to be especially at risk for respiratory diseases as they were used to going up into the cold and snow of the high mountains. We didn't know that then and didn't want to take any chances.

Mealtimes were interesting. We were all having meals together in a common dining room. Santiago and Wenceslao were trying to do everything right. They tried to do as they saw the others doing. The first morning they cut up their toast with their knives and forks and ate it with their forks. They were just getting the hang of all the utensils when one meal they sat by a man from South Africa who had a different technique altogether. That really confused them. The Kogis were not at all finicky and ate everything that was offered to them.

True to his word, Santiago was willing to answer all the questions that Chad asked him about the language and culture. Chad was able to complete a word list for comparison with other languages and make a start on language learning. The language seemed as strange as everything else about the

Kogis. It was not like anything we had studied at the Institute of Linguistics. As the week drew to an end, Santiago voiced the words we had been waiting to hear. "You have been so kind to me, I want to return the hospitality. You can come and visit me and stay up to three weeks. Chad had told me that one of the other Kogi families in the area had two houses, so I suggested that we could stay in one of Miguel's houses. (I didn't know then that traditionally there were two houses on every Kogi farm, one for the men and one for the women.) I didn't know either that this Miguel was Santiago's life-long rival, the one who had every chance but didn't bother to learn. It was evident that Santiago did not like this idea. *He* would build us a house on *his* farm, he insisted.

When the week was over, Chad bundled the Kogis back onto the airplane. They were loaded down with gifts. They each had large dolls for their daughters, beads for their wives, and tennis shoes and Colombian *ruanas*, woolen ponchos that would serve as blankets for the cool nights in the Sierra. Santiago's smile was big as he said goodbye. He promised to start building our house right away.

Chapter 23

Life at Lomalinda

In a few days we would leave for Lomalinda. I called the clinic where Gloria was born and talked with the head nurse. "What can I give my five-week-old baby, so she won't get malaria?" I asked her. I knew there was preventive medicine for adults and older children, but I also knew it was toxic, and I wasn't sure at all that it could be given to such a small baby. I also knew that malaria was rampant in the *Llanos,* the eastern plains where Lomalinda was located.

"Why would you want to give malaria medicine to such a small baby?" the nurse wanted to know. This was not Annie Noble, but the very efficient and businesslike Marion Price, the head of the whole clinic.

"Because we are going out to Lomalinda?" was my timid answer. I always felt intimidated by Marion, a woman capable of running an entire clinic.

"My advice is to not take your baby into such a risky situation," replied Marion. "There is nothing that you can give her. Why do you want to do such a thing?"

There was no way I could explain to single lady, Marion, that I was not making a capricious decision to put my child at risk. How could I explain in taking two minutes of her busy time, our call to missions, our commitment to Wycliffe, and our need to get out of the expensive living of Bogotá while Santiago was building a house for us? All I could do was hopelessly mumble something about Wycliffe building their base in the *Llanos*. I was very happy to be able to hang up the telephone.

Many Colombian city people in Bogotá had warned us about taking our children to the *Llanos*. There are *tigres* (jaguars) out there, we were told. We were also warned about boa constrictors and their water counterparts, anacondas. The lakes were full of piranhas, flesh-eating fish. We were also told that there were big birds that could swoop down and carry off a small child. The lake where Lomalinda was being built was noted for being the home of a water monster. If we had not been through Jungle Camp, and if Chad and the boys had not already spent several months out there, we might have been intimidated. As it was, it was only the prevalence of malaria that really worried me. We had been taught about this disease in our clinic classes at Jungle Camp, and I really didn't want any of us to get it. I knew that once infected, it could become a reoccurring, life-long problem. It seemed that Sharon had already been infected at Jungle Camp.

Nevertheless, one day in early November, we headed for Lomalinda. I don't remember how we traveled to Villavicencio, but at the airstrip there, we were met by the JAARS plane and flown to Lomalinda. JAARS, Jungle Aviation and Radio Service, was the air and radio arm of the Wycliffe Bible Translators. Their members were integrated with the rest of us but were there to provide transportation to and from the tribal locations and to keep in radio contact with all of us translators. About this time, we were told that we were supposed to have $500 to contribute to the radio part of the ministry. This information should have come to us before we left home, but was another thing we never got.

It was decided that easy payments could be taken out of our slim monthly income.

From the air, Lomalinda consisted of six small cabins clustered on a plateau above the lake, surrounded by rolling hills, thus the name, L o m a l i n d a , beautiful hills. One family had already started building their permanent house a little distance from the cabins.

Behind our cabin two single translator ladies were also building a small house that looked like a mansion compared to the small cabin where our family would be living. A washhouse was also in the construction stage, centrally located in the middle of the cabins. At the present, however, sanitary facilities were postholes out behind the cabins, a semblance of privacy was provided by straw mats hung on at least three sides. Water was pumped from the lake and was almost the color of coffee without bothering to make the coffee. Chad had purchased a four-burner apartment-sized gas stove with an oven, and a small sink set into a small cabinet. He had made a kitchen worktable along one side of the cabin, ending in order to allow the head of the boys' bunk bed to occupy the rest of that wall. The foot of that bed stretched to the door. On the other side of the door was the head of the double bed; complete with the foam rubber mattress we had brought in three pieces all the way from Minnesota. At the foot of the double bed was the baby's crib. Across the back wall, from the crib to the stove was the aluminum folding cot for Sharon, also brought from Minnesota.

As we were preparing to leave for Colombia, my mother had bought the cot for Sharon. "I don't know where the rest of you are going to sleep," said Mother, "But I want my granddaughter to have a decent bed." Chad had built the bunk beds and crib in Bogotá and brought them out on a truck. We also had a beautiful wooden Cape Cod style rocking chair that was made by Indians at the Wycliffe base in Peru. It just fit in a little space between the foot of our bed, Sharon's cot, and the crib. Right in the middle of the room was a table. This was a very special table. It would seat six comfortably, and more could be crowded in. It was made out of plywood with some kind of aluminum legs that were individually screwed into the plywood. It never wobbled. It had the capacity to adjust itself to any kind of uneven floor. Later we took it to the tribe where we enjoyed it for many

years. We purchased four kitchen chairs and several round stools.

A shelf in the corner over the crib held our tape recorder, and several other shelves in corners held essentials such as towels, sheets, and personal items. Each one of us had a colorful cloth hanging-bag with pockets. I made these in Bogotá while waiting for Gloria's birth. Russell's was blue, Chaddy's green, Sharon's pink, Gloria's pink and aqua blue, and Chad's navy. For the life of me I can't remember what color mine was, but I know I had one. It probably was made of scraps from some of the others. Anyway, these were very useful items. Across the top were small pockets, especially sized for toothbrush, toothpaste, hairbrush or comb, pen, pencil, flashlight, deodorant, etc. The middle row contained mid-sized pockets for underwear, etc. The bottom row consisted of two large pockets with elastic in the top of each one for larger items, such as pajamas and bathing suits.

These bags each had a strategic place on the wall near the owner's sleeping area. They were invaluable in keeping order in such crowded quarters, and later on, each one was folded over and put into a duffel bag for the trip to the tribe. Upon arrival they were hung up again, and all was in order. In addition, Chad had bought a metal footlocker for each of the children. These fit under the beds unless pulled out to provide additional seating space, and held shoes, jeans, and larger clothing items. Between the bags and the footlockers the children had a place to keep all their treasures. Chad and I had more trouble with our belongings, as our clothes were larger, and we had to fit everything on shelves.

The first trips to Lomalinda had been in the heat of the dry season, and the cabins had been planned with screening on all sides to catch all the breeze possible. Now in the rainy season, this was a problem. Every family had a different idea of handling the situation. Chad had hung straw mats from ropes up over the top boards of the cabin. By pulling on the ropes from inside, we could raise up the mats to cover the windows, and then lower them for light and ventilation when the rain stopped. This system worked well except that the mats looked rather strange when viewed from the outside. Chad had also rigged up a rainwater system so that we could drink rainwater from the roof rather than the coffee-colored lake water. (Of course, we boiled it first.)

We slept under mosquito nets in order to lessen the chance of getting malaria. One advantage in the *Llanos* was that the air cooled off quickly after the sun went down around 6:00 p.m.. We slept under sheets and light blankets. The patchwork quilts I had made for each of the children while I was waiting for Gloria's arrival turned out to be just the right covers for Lomalinda. The mosquito nets were not oppressive as I had thought they would be, and they gave a bit of privacy in the one-room cabin.

Somehow the group had gotten a hold of two old-style Maytag wringer washers and some washtubs. We women were assigned washing times each week, and mothers got double time. We had to sort our wash and plan how to get it through the washer and rinse tubs in one load of water. Even though the water was dark brown, the clothes came out surprisingly white. Afterwards we hung the clothes on lines stretched between poles erected around the washhouse where the hot tropical sun bleached out any clinging stain. The laundry side of the washhouse was operational, but the bathrooms and showers were still under construction. Bathing was done in the lake, taking your chances with the piranhas. The reason that washing machine time and water was so limited was that our small electric generator was only run for two or three hours in the morning and another two in the afternoon. That meant that only four or five women could wash in one day. There was plenty of water in the lake, but only so much could be pumped during the hours of electricity.

An all purpose kitchen, dining room, tabernacle building was also under construction. I forgot to mention that the cabins were built up off the ground with a crawl space underneath and had floors made of wooden boards. Russell and Chaddy were the official termite inspectors. They crawled under the cabins periodically with flashlights, looking for termite nests. I'm not sure what they did if they found any. We used the crawl space near the door of the cabin for storing cases of canned goods that we had brought from Bogotá. I also kept the dirty clothes and diapers in suitable plastic containers under the house awaiting washday.

School had been transferred from Bogotá to Lomalinda about the same time that we made the move. Kathy had been sent to San Martin to teach the children of a family that was operating the Wycliffe house there, so Isabel Kerr was the teacher of all the children at Lomalinda. By this time Chaddy loved school, so Isabel told me she was going to put the pressure on him to learn to read, and if I thought it was too much to let her know. In a few weeks, Chaddy was reading fluently. Isabel was also the camp nurse. She lived alone in one of the cabins awaiting the arrival of her translation partner, so her cabin also became the infirmary and health clinic. Isabel was and is a tremendous person and gave me much emotional and spiritual support in all these first difficult months in Colombia.

Chad was working on the roof of the small house being built near the cabin. Somehow he fell off, but his fall was broken by a taut rope. He ended up with a twisted ankle and broken ribs from hitting the rope. Now that we were in hot country, Gloria only wore a diaper and a little shirt, and everyone was commenting on her left leg. It really turned in in a most unnatural position. Then in a few days I developed a severe toothache in one of my back molars. Isabel was treating me with aspirin for toothache and Chad for his ankle and ribs. After a few days she said, "Why don't you two go back to Bogotá to get yourselves treated. I'll take care of the school children for you, but take the baby with you."

"That's great," I agreed, "I want to have the baby's leg checked again anyway."

Chapter 24

Dark Days

Bogotá
Nov. 1964

Medical appointments had been made for us by the Bogotá staff before we arrived in Bogotá. That very afternoon, my aching molar was extracted, and in the morning Chad saw a doctor. His broken ribs were taped and his ankle treated. Gloria's appointment with a pediatric specialist was scheduled for the afternoon. This doctor had been trained in Texas and spoke excellent English. This time he examined her hips. "She's got all the signs of a congenital hip dislocation," he told us. "She will probably have to wear a pillow splint for a few months. Don't worry, she's never going to be a great athlete, but after a few months in a pillow splint, she will be just fine." He ordered X-rays taken and told us to pick up the X-rays the next day and bring them to his office.

That evening was our last time of peace before the blow fell. The next morning we sent a radio message to Lomalinda, saying that we would be delayed a few days. When we arrived at the X-ray department of the hospital, the doctor was there waiting for us with Gloria's X-rays in his hand and a grim look on his face. "She's got it in the third degree," he told us. He sent us immediately to the office of a colleague, an orthopedic specialist. This doctor had been trained in France. He was fluent in French and German, as well as Spanish, but this didn't help us any. In desperation in trying to communicate, he handed us an English medical book opened to the page that told about Gloria's condition. From the book I understood that this was a hereditary condition, carried by the male, but almost always seen in females. A mild untreated case resulted in prominent hips, feet turned in, and a distinctive "duck walk." I thought at once of my dad's aunts. This description fit them to a tee. The doctor continued to talk, and I understood the words, traction, cast, and a Catholic hospital for crippled children. We could go back to Lomalinda, he said, and he would put Gloria in the children's hospital. The treatment would be long-term, he warned us.

At this point I couldn't take it anymore. I ran out of the doctor's office crying, with Gloria in my arms. Chad stayed to hear the doctor out and read the medical book. Then he joined me in one of the lounge areas of the hospital. I was desperate. I had heard of the terrible care that was given to children in these hospitals. How could I abandon my two-month-old-baby to strangers and return to the *Llanos*? Maybe Miss Annie can help us, Chad remarked.

We returned to the Wycliffe Group House and called Annie Noble. She said she would talk with Marion Price and get back to us. Soon Marion called asking for the name of the doctor. She wanted us to transfer the care of Gloria to the orthopedic specialist who worked out of that clinic, but we didn't want to do so. I can't imagine why we didn't at least ask for a second opinion, but we were now sadly in the red. The mission finance office kept giving us the cash we needed to pay the bills, but we knew we were in bad shape. Since the clinic doctor had not been able to diagnose Gloria's problem, it didn't seem that their orthopedist would be much better. We felt like we should at least stick with the doctors who had found her problem. I had also read in the medical book that the treatment would have been merely a matter of days instead of months, if the condition had been caught at birth.

The next day Annie called again. Marion had arranged everything with the doctor. Gloria and I would be admitted to the WEC clinic and given a private room. The doctor would come all the way across Bogotá to put her into traction. I could stay with Gloria in the hospital room and take care of her. Chad could go back to Lomalinda to be with the other children. This was actually a great concession for the busy doctor to travel all across town to attend Gloria. Annie and Marion had worked a miracle.

We arrived at the clinic and were installed in a stark, white, windowless room, clean, but devoid of any decoration or amenities. There was a bed for me and a crib for Gloria. I could have meals in the nurses' dining room, I was told. Soon the doctor arrived with lumber, a saw, ropes and who knows what else. Lots of jokes were passed between him and Marion as to looking more like a carpenter than a doctor. The two bottom legs of the crib were elevated, and Gloria's legs were attached to ropes that went up over the foot of the crib. Weights were attached to the other end of the ropes. Her upper body was attached to the head of the crib. The object was to bring the left femur down into position. Since the pelvis had no hip socket, the bone was too high up in the body. Gloria wailed incessantly, but no one but me seemed to care. How I longed to hold her in my arms and comfort her. I tried to give her the baby bottle, but she refused it. She would be in this position four days, the doctor told me, then one day in a different position, and then she would be put into a cast. After the cast was on, I could take her home.

Gloria napped fitfully but mostly just wailed, to me a heartrending cry for help. I leaned over the crib, stroking her body and trying to comfort her. Finally Miss Annie had a chair brought in so I could sit beside the crib. As I sat there disconsolately in the bare, windowless room, I mentally reviewed the last few months. This definitely was not what I had in mind when I answered the call to missions. I was mentally prepared to slog through mud and live in the boonies Jungle Camp style to bring the gospel to an unreached tribe, but I was not prepared for this. What had gone wrong? Where was God in all this? We had prayed for Gloria's healing. Why didn't God act? If I could only get word to my prayer group in Minneapolis. If only Pastor Hegre and Pastor Brokke, the pastors at Bethany, would pray for Gloria, I knew she would be instantly healed like Sharon was when she had malaria in Minneapolis.

When Gloria dozed off about noon, I ran upstairs to the nurse's dining room. What a welcome break to sit in the tastefully decorated little dining room, drinking tea from colorful English bone china cups with Miss Annie. But when I returned to my dungeon, Gloria was crying again. This continued all night. By morning, I felt like a wrung out dishrag. Miss Annie called the doctor, and he prescribed a liquid called *Infastress*. This was a tranquilizer and pain remedy that could be used with babies. This was a great find, and I used it many times later in the tribe when some unpleasant procedure had to be performed on babies or toddlers. With the *Infastress* Gloria calmed down and slept more, and I was able to get up to the nurse's dining room to eat and to visit while one of the student nurses kept an eye on Gloria.

One day Miss Annie asked if I could help her. It happened that she had been asked to sing a solo at the student nurses' graduation, and she needed help reading the words of the hymn she wanted to sing. Miss Annie had very bad eyesight. She wore both contact lenses and heavy glasses. She had just received new contacts, but had to wait several days for new lenses to be put into the frames of her eyeglasses. That morning she had insisted that I walk with her to the nearby apartment where she and Marion Price lived together with another missionary lady. It was wonderful to get out into the sunshine again. I was very uneasy about leaving Gloria, but Annie insisted that I stay long enough for a piece of pie that she had baked herself the day before. She had obvious trouble getting the pie from the pan to the plate. In fact, it landed on the kitchen counter. "I hope you get your glasses back before you have to deliver a baby," I remarked. "Humph," responded Annie, "I've already received two this morning. I can do that with my eyes shut." (In Colombia, the attendants don't 'deliver' the baby, they just 'receive' it.)

After lunch, Annie brought out the Spanish hymnal and opened it to her song. To my delight, it was a hymn that I knew in English and that had meant a lot to me in the days before we came to Colombia. I was surprised at the rich quality of Annie's voice as she started the first stanza. (She sang in Spanish, but I am going to give you the English version.)

I traveled down a lonely road,
And no one seemed to care.
The burden on my weary back
Had bowed me to despair
I oft complained to Jesus,
How folks were treating me,
And then I heard Him say
so tenderly,

"My feet were also weary
Upon the Calvary road.
The cross became so heavy,
I fell beneath the load.
Be faithful weary pilgrim,
The morning I can see,
Just lift your cross,
And follow close to me."

Annie knew the first stanza, but she wanted me to help her learn the other two. Even though in Spanish, the words spoke to my heart.

"I work so hard for Jesus,"
I often boast and say,
"I've sacrificed a lot of things
to walk the narrow way.
I gave up fame and fortune,
I'm worth a lot to Thee,"
And then I hear Him
gently say to me,

Part Three: The Making of a Missionary

"I left the throne of glory
And counted it as loss,
My hands were nailed in anger
Upon a cruel cross,
But now we'll make the journey
With your hand safe in Mine,
So lift your cross
And follow close to Me.

Oh, Jesus, if I die upon
A foreign field some day,
'Twould be no more
than love demands,
No less could I repay,
"No greater love hath mortal man
Than for a friend to die"
These are the words He
gently spoke to me,

Several lines stood out to me in the last stanza:

"If just a cup of water,
I place within your hand;
Then just a cup of water,
Is all that I demand,"
But if by death to living
They can Thy glory see,
I'll take my cross and follow
Close to Thee.

Hymn – Follow Me by Ira F. Stanphil, 1953

Annie learned her hymn, and I was refreshed in my spirit.
The Lord knew what was going on. He knew my heart. He
knew I couldn't do heroic exploits for Him right now. He
had placed this little suffering baby in my hand, and I would
relinquish her to His care and do the best I could.

But this was the calm before the storm.

Chapter 25

Darker Days

The next morning the doctor returned for the second step of Gloria's treatment.

This time the ropes, weights, and pulleys were moved to each side of the crib, and the baby's legs were pulled outwards. Although I had given her a dose of *Infastress* before the doctor's arrival, as soon as the weights were hung in the new position, Gloria's wails turned to screams of pain. She was obviously being hurt very badly. Nothing I could do would help. She had been drinking her bottles, but now she refused them again. Annie Nobel tried to comfort me. "As soon as the doctor puts her in the cast, she will be fine, and you can hold her." (X-rays much later showed that something went wrong at this point and the neck of Gloria's left femur was twisted by the weights.)

This was one of the longest days of my life. Towards evening Annie called the doctor. Soon he was there. After examining Gloria, he decided to put on the cast right away. They carried Gloria, crib and all, to the operating room, or wherever they do the casts. I was left alone in my white dungeon. I had no idea what they were doing to my baby, but I held on to Annie's words that as soon as the cast was on, she would be better.

I lay down on the hard, narrow bed. I closed my eyes and prayed for whatever was going on upstairs with Gloria. The cold was damp and penetrating in this interior room where the sunshine never entered. After what seemed like hours, a movement in the corridor alerted me that Gloria was returning. Annie Nobel marched in proudly, and laid my baby beside me.

But what a shock! Gloria's body was encased in wet plaster from her armpits to her toes. She had been given a general anesthetic and looked like she was dead. Her face was as white as the plaster cast. Her hands were as cold as ice. I went into shock myself. Annie brought in an electric heater, assigned a student nurse to stay with Gloria, and put me to bed with some kind of a sleeping potion.

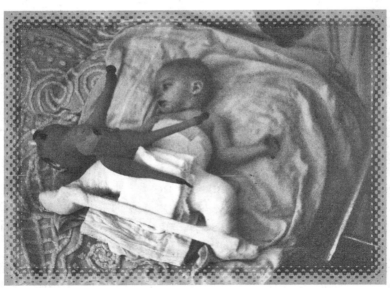

The next morning Gloria and I were put into a taxi and sent back to the Wycliffe Group House. Either that day or the next was the American Thanksgiving. There was a handful of people in the group house, and they invited me to join them for a special turkey dinner. They were very kind, but none of them were people I knew very well as yet, and I was terribly lonely. Gloria had of course regained consciousness, but she was still miserable and very fussy.   She was in her own little prison of plaster, cut off from human touch and warmth. Annie said she would be better when the cast dried out. I was exhausted. I was worn out physically and emotionally. News came from Lomalinda. The new dining hall was in use, and a wonderful Thanksgiving dinner was enjoyed by all, including a number of Indians who had been brought to the base from the jungle as language helpers. I thought of Chad and my other children and wished I could have been with them. I was very depressed, cold, and lonely.

I don't know how many days went by, but all of a sudden, Chad was there. I have never been happier to see him. A pastor friend from Minnesota, Spencer Bower, had been at Lomalinda as the speaker for our first conference. Somehow he sensed the situation and paid Chad's way to come back to be with me, and Isabel had been willing to stay with our other children again. Our account was now so in the red that we didn't dare spend any money expect for the most basic necessities. Once Chad arrived, I really did collapse. I slept the clock around while he cared for Gloria. However when I woke up again, I was recuperated and back to normal, ready to take on the responsibility for Gloria's care. We started to make plans to return to Lomalinda with the baby.

One of the first things we did was to write letters home telling our parents, the pastors at Bethany, the ladies in my prayer group, and all our friends and supporters what had happened. I was so sure that when our friends in the States started praying, Gloria would be instantly healed.

Chad realized that I was going to need help when I returned to Lomalinda. He went to a Colombian pastor that he knew, and he asked if there was a teen-aged girl in his church who would be willing to come to work for us and help me, especially with Gloria. The pastor said he knew just the girl. Chad went back to Lomalinda and built a little lean-to on the backside of the cabin. By the time he returned for us,

Gloria was getting used to her cast, and it was getting very close to Christmas. This would be our first Christmas with just our family since 1957, and we were looking forward to it. We bought one present for each child. I remember that for Sharon, Chad found a life-sized baby doll that looked just like Gloria, except for the cast of course.

This time we traveled by taxi. (You have to remember that in Colombia, as in most South American countries, travel by taxi is just a little more expensive than by bus and is much cheaper than maintaining your own vehicle.) I remember that Gloria lay on the back seat in her cast, and whenever we were stopped, which was often, people stared in the window and remarked that the Christmas baby was in the car. The white cast looked like "swaddling clothes" to them. At Villavicencio, we were once again met by the JAARS airplane and flown to Lomalinda.

The children were happy to see us and their baby sister. Many changes had taken place at Lomalinda while I was gone. In addition to the dining hall, the bathrooms in the washhouse were finished and usable. The small house behind us was finished, and part of it was used as a school. A few more family homes had been built. A large building was being constructed where school children could stay while their parents went to the tribal areas. Regular Sunday Services were being held in the dining hall, and the different men took turns preaching. On Sunday evenings we heard reports from the tribal teams that had returned.

As Christmas drew near, we started receiving Christmas mail from our friends in the United States. (The mail was delivered to the Wycliffe Post Office Box in Bogotá, and then flown out to Lomalinda on the JAARS flights. We had a little post office building at Lomalinda with a 'pigeon hole' for each family.) To our great surprise, almost every Christmas card contained a small check for our Christmas. We rushed them over to the finance office and deposited them to our account. Soon we were out of the red. All the extra medical expenses had been met.

Several of the missionary families were very sad about spending their first Christmas far from their loved ones. Many expressed regret about the lack of snow and the normal U.S. hustle and bustle, lights, evergreens, church Christmas programs, etc. As  a group we sang Christmas Carols in the dining hall, shared Christmas baking, (I think the school had a small children's program), and did the best we could to generate some Yuletide cheer. However no one could change the fact that we were into the dry season, the hottest time of the year.

On Christmas Eve we found an interestingly shaped branch, covered it with white cotton in good Colombian fashion, and decorated it with colored balls. We set it up in a little space by the door. In the evening on the 24th we sang Christmas carols, read the Christmas story, and opened the presents. For us it was a fine Christmas. In the morning we had a special breakfast and the children each had a Christmas stocking to open with candy and small gifts. Alba fit in well with the family. She was 16 years old and still a kid at heart.

Alba and I had a fairly hard time communicating. I had memorized phrases such as: Wash the dishes, sweep the floor, peel the potatoes, etc. With Alba's help I had enough time free to attend informal Spanish classes that were being held by one of the older missionary ladies from Peru. I learned more practical Spanish in these classes and communicating with Alba than I had at the University of the Andes.

Chapter 26

A Cup of Cold Water

Lomalinda,
January, 1965

Little by little I was able to communicate more with Alba. Her father had been killed in the recent violence, she told me, and her mother had died of cancer. She lived with her brother and his family in Bogotá. She had wanted to run away and get married when she was 14, but her brother had beaten her with a belt, and she had given up the idea. She seemed to think he had done the right thing. Many girls want to get married at that age, she told me. If the family gets the upper hand, they give up the idea. Now Alba was interested in studying. She had wanted to start at the Bible Institute run by the denomination that her brother's church belonged to (WEC), but they had just raised their minimum age to 17. Since she was only 16, she would have to wait another year. She admitted to being a handful for her brother and sister-in-law to handle, so he was probably happy to have her come to Lomalinda with us. Being from Bogotá, she was worried about jaguars and demanded that a door with a secure bolt be added to her "room" (the lean-to).

Alba probably wouldn't have made it as a "maid" in any other family, but she was willing and able to do the few things I required of her. She swept the floor, washed the dishes, hung the diapers, and did some simple vegetable preparation. She could also hold Gloria if she got fussy while I was cooking. Chad felt she should take parasite medicine if she was going to be involved in our food preparation, but it turned out that she was sure she couldn't swallow a pill. The nurse stocked some very sweet, sticky syrup that was effective against roundworm, a common parasite in Colombia. Chad decided that would do. One Saturday after breakfast he gave a spoonful each to Sharon, Russell, and Chaddy; then he tried to give one to Alba, but she wouldn't have it. "It's for your *culebras*," he told her. Now parasites are called either *lombrices* or *gusanos,* but *culebras* is the word for "snakes." This made Alba snicker, but she still wouldn't take the medicine. Out the door she went with Chad right behind her. Round and round the cabin she ran with Chad right behind her with the bottle of medicine and the spoon shouting, "For your *culebras,* for your *culebras."* Finally, since she was laughing so hard she couldn't run anymore, she stopped and took the medicine.

It was hard to get along without a refrigerator, but Isabel let me keep our meat in her refrigerator. Sjaan Waller gave me a tray of ice cubes everyday at noon to cool down our lemonade. Lomalinda had a small electric generator, and we were severely rationed as to electricity. The generator ran from 6 to 9 at night, and two hours in the morning and two in the afternoon. This kept the meat from spoiling, although it kept thawing and refreezing. Vegetables came once a week and I learned to use the more perishable ones, like lettuce and cauliflower first and leave the cabbage, carrots, and beets until the end of the week. We all went to bed at 9:00 p.m. when the lights went out.

Unbeknownst to me, Chad wrote to my parents in Minneapolis and told them that we were the only family in Lomalinda without a refrigerator. He also told them about the electricity problem. Dad located a large, bottle-gas refrigerator and sent it down with another missionary family that was coming from Minneapolis. Mother and Dad did not want to give us monthly support to sustain us in Colombia, but if we were going to be there anyway, they wanted to help make life more comfortable for us. What a happy day it was for me when the large gas refrigerator was delivered to our door. Somehow we made room for it between the foot of Sharon's bed and the stove. Once hooked up, it worked like a charm. We had plenty of storage space for all our vegetables and meat, and made lots of ice cubes.

About this time my sister sent us all her children's outgrown clothes. She had two boys older than Russell and a girl between Sharon and Gloria in age. None of the clothes fit at the moment, so we packed them in our empty barrels that we had had shipped from Minneapolis. Then we stacked the barrels to make a water tower. Water was pumped from the lake into a cement storage tank that we had placed on top of the barrels, and the height of our tower gave us good water pressure in our kitchen sink. A second cement tank caught rainwater, which we used for drinking and cooking. One of my prayers was that the Lord would keep water in the rain barrel all through the dry season so I wouldn't have to use the brown lake water in the baby's bottle.

From the time we returned to Lomalinda with the baby, we started having a lot of visitors. Rural Colombian people lived all around the base on the side away from the lake and towards the town of Puerto Lleras. One of their main recreations was to visit Lomalinda and see all the funny things the gringos did. A number of the men worked at Lomalinda as manual laborers or in construction, carpentry, etc. Chad had been their boss when he was out at Lomalinda in the early days with the boys. The children of these families came to our door frequently. They were fascinated with Gloria and liked to play with all her toys. After they were gone, I had to gather up all the toys and disinfect them. I didn't want her catching parasites from their grimy little hands.

After our refrigerator arrived, the children started coming to the door more often. They also started asking for a glass of water. Of course they meant cold water out of the refrigerator, preferable with an ice cube or two. I didn't realize that I could give them just one big glass and they would all share it as they did in their homes. I gave each one of them their own glass of water with an ice cube it. Some of the women on the base mentioned that this was a big bother, and they were trying to discourage the habit. Yes, it was a bother. Especially since when they left I had to wash all the glasses with soap and scald them with boiling water (as we had been taught in Jungle Camp.) But the weather was hot and dusty. They had walked quite a ways from their homes where there were no refrigerators either.

I really cared for these children. I longed to share Jesus with them, but my Spanish vocabulary was just too deficient. Then when I was really getting frustrated, a song went through my mind:

> If just a cup of water,
> I hold within my hand;
> Then just a cup of water
> Is all that I demand.

Suddenly, the whole situation changed. I was giving that glass of water in the name of the Lord. Then a verse came to mind:

> And whosoever shall give to drink unto one of these little ones a cup of **cold** water . . . verily I say unto you, he shall in no wise lose his reward. Matthew 10:42

I noticed that the verse said **cold** water. How did people in the Holy Land get *cold water?* I wondered. It must have been much harder for them than simply taking it out of a refrigerator. At any rate, the "cold water ministry" became a joy instead of a grudging act.

Chapter 27

Bad News

The time passed quickly. Soon it was time to take Gloria back to her doctor in Bogotá. This time Chad stayed with the children, and Edna Hedland, a translator to the Tunebo tribe, accompanied me. She was fluent in Spanish and would be able to interpret for me and was a Registered Nurse as well.

The doctor took X-rays; then he called us into his office. "There has been no improvement," he told us sadly. I think she will have to have surgery. He explained that since there was no bone in Gloria's little body suitable for a bone graft, they would have to run tests on both parents to see which one of us was the best match. Then a piece of bone would be removed from one of us and grafted into Gloria's hip to make a socket. Since there was only a 30% chance that the graft would "take," the doctor wanted us to go back to the States for the operation. "I could do it here, but if it doesn't work she will be in a wheelchair for the rest of her life. You will say, 'Why did we have this surgery done down here in the middle of South America?' If you were French, I would send you back to France. If you were German, I would send you back to Germany. Since you are Americans, you need to return to the United States," the doctor explained. Then he added, "You will have to stay under the care of the doctor who does the surgery for at least three years."

"How long can we wait before we have to make this decision?" I asked the doctor through Edna.

"Oh, you can wait another two months," the doctor responded. Then he took Gloria down to the cast room to replace her old cast with a new one.

Somehow the placement of this cast was not as traumatic as the first one had been. She was now 5 months old and better able to stand the stress. However, it took a day for the new cast to dry out. In the room that had been assigned to us at the Group House, she lay in a small crib in the corner, while I tried to mentally cope with the new blow that had been dealt us. Our friends at home had received the news. They had sent letters saying that they were praying for Gloria. Pastor Hegre himself had written. He mentioned something about "the trial of our faith." We were in a room occupied by some of our friends who were on vacation in another part of Colombia for a few days. I had requested a radio appointment with Chad and was waiting for the appointed hour to arrive. Assisted by a good dose of *Infastress*, the baby dozed off.

It seemed that the hand of the Lord had been so evident in bringing us to Colombia. An invitation to the Kogi tribe had been extended by Santiago. Further research revealed what a miracle that had been. It seemed that no outsider had ever been allowed to even stay overnight in one of their villages. Their usual greeting to the few government officials or others that ventured into their area was, "When are you leaving?" The Lord had provided an open door through Santiago. Were we now going to be prevented from walking through it?

The time for my appointment with Chad drew near. I left Gloria sleeping and went downstairs. I repeated to him all that the doctor had said. Of course this was a great disappointment to him and the children, as we were all highly motivated to go to live with Santiago. We agreed to spend time that evening seeking the Lord and set a time to talk again the next day.

After a quick supper, I returned to the room to find Gloria still asleep. After praying and sensing the presence of the Lord, I looked at the bookcase where my friends who normally lived in that room had left some of their books. I had not brought my own Bible, so I randomly pulled out one of theirs. It was a small, hard-covered Bible portion. At the time I thought it was a part of the Amplified Bible that was then being released several books at a time. I had earnestly been asking the Lord to guide me by giving me a special word from the Bible. I opened the small book, and a verse fairly leapt out at me.

Do not return to your own country.

These were the words that burned themselves into my heart. Years later, I vainly searched for this verse. I couldn't even find the reference with the aid of an Exhaustive Concordance. It was a modern translation and probably was worded differently in the King James. At the time, however, I was so confident that the Lord had spoken, that I didn't even look for the verse again. After much reflection I have decided that it must have been a part of the word given to the wise men. Something like, *Do not return to your own country by the same way.* However be it as it may, this was God's word to me that evening. The peace of God reigned in my heart as I lay down to go to sleep.

In the morning Chad and I talked again. He had received a similar message from the Lord. We decided that I would return to Lomalinda with the baby, and we would pray for two months, and then bring her in again, hoping for signs of progress.

Chapter 28

Dry Season

We had been back at Lomalinda for several weeks. We were now in the height of the dry season. A stiff wind blew all day, dissipating the heat somewhat, but drying out a person's entire body. I gave thanks for the refrigerator and the ever-present supply of ice cubes. Although I had to start boiling lake water for drinking and kitchen use, we saved the fast dwindling rain water for Gloria's bottles. It was kind of disconcerting to find brown sediment in the bottom of the drinking water pitcher every day as well as in the bottom of each ice cube tray. I certainly didn't want Gloria drinking this sediment in her baby bottle.

The intense heat and strong wind were debilitating, and the rain water supply would be gone in a few days. I intensified my prayers for rain. The women who had lived at Lomalinda from the beginning told me about the *chuascos*, heavy rains accompanied by extremely strong winds. In Bogotá the people referred to these storms in the *Llanos* as "hurricanes." This was another reason that Bogotános feared the *Llanos*. The women told me that at the last conference (I was in Bogotá with the baby) one of these storms had come up while everyone was in the dining hall with bowls of soup served. They claimed that the wind blew the soup right out of the bowls. All the first buildings at Lomalinda were built for the hot weather. The walls were mostly screening with no way to close them against the occasional heavy rains. Once a *chuasco* got going, rain could be blown horizontally right through a building. The only comparatively dry place was under the tables. Also, during a *chuasco* storm the wind would change direction, eventually coming from all four points of the compass before the storm subsided. The women told of having to all go out into the heavy rain and wind of a *chuasco* to add their weight to that of the men to keep the little JAARS airplane from being blown over and damaged by the *chuasco*. By the time I went out to Lomalinda to live, secure cement tie-downs had been installed for the airplane.

But now in the middle of the dry season, everything was dry as a bone and hot as a desert. I finally had to admit

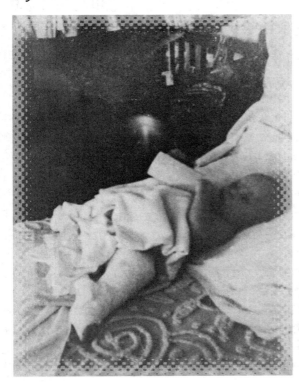

that I had come to the end of the rainwater. I boiled lake water and let it settle several times in several different containers to try to settle out all the brown sediment. All of the Latin American countries that I have been in have a very excellent powdered whole milk that comes in cans. Our family used a five pound can a week. We raised Gloria on this powdered milk, but possibly at this time she was still on a powdered infant formula. At any rate, I had to give her her evening bottle made of the water from the lake. Try as I might, there was still brown sediment in the bottom of her bottle.

It seemed like we had just gotten to sleep when the storm hit. Chad, who had endured these *chuascos* before, jumped up and pulled up the straw mats to cover the windows. That helped but did not shut out all the wind and rain. A certain amount of water was driven through the cracks in the mats. A fine spray entered under the eaves and showered the whole house. Before it was over, the rain came through every side of the little cabin. The boys and Sharon were wide-awake, rejoicing in the cool wetness of the night after the days of intensive dry heat. I had to keep Gloria and her cast dry through all this, so I had to put her under the table, the only dry place in the house. There was a blessing in all this though; I could imagine our rain barrel full and overflowing with sparkling clean rainwater.

At last the storm was over. The beds were all damp, but so were the extra sheets that were on a shelf. I did find dry sheets and blankets for Gloria in her footlocker. We all tumbled back to bed for what remained of the night. In the morning we all enjoyed the milk mixed with clear, cool rainwater, and Gloria never had to have another lake-water bottle again. The Lord kept our rain barrel full by sending periodic *chuascos* all the rest of the dry season. (I don't believe there was another dry season in the *Llanos* in the memory of any of us that had so many *chuascos* during a dry season.)

After the *chuasco* the days turned very hot, and Gloria became very fussy. We tried all the usual means of making her happy to no avail. The *Infastress* helped, but I tried to only give it to her at night so we could all get some sleep. The heat intensified. We all took turns holding Gloria, but she would not be comforted. I started noticing a very disagreeable odor about her. Since Peggy Wheeler had returned from the tribe, Isabel had become a full time teacher, and Peggy took over the nursing duties. I called for her help, and we decided that maybe some fecal material had gotten into the cotton under her cast. (In each of her casts, a "window" had been cut out so that I could diaper her.) We pulled out the cotton around the window and restuffed it with clean cotton. That did not seem to help the problem. The next day was even worse. Visitors started dropping in having heard that there was a problem with Gloria. All of them noticed the disagreeable odor which was getting stronger all the time. I believe it was Isabel who remarked, "You don't suppose that she has sores under her cast, do you?"

I knew at once that that was the problem. I sent for Peggy, and she too felt like that must be the problem. "We will have to cut a "window" in the cast," Peggy told me, "So we can see what her skin looks like under the cast." We started sniffing the cast to locate the spot of the strongest odor. By now the men were home from work. Chad went to get someone who had a special saw that might be able to cut a window in the cast. On Peggy's advice, I gave Gloria a double dose of *Infastress*. Cutting a window in the cast proved to be a difficult task. The children came home and with wide eyes ate the supper that Alba served them and quietly crawled under their mosquito nets to silently watch what was happening to their baby sister. Before the task was done, we had six different men and six different saws working on the hole one after another.

When the piece of plaster cast was finally loose, Gloria's compressed skin bulged out through the hole. It was oozing and covered with sores. Someone went to arrange an emergency flight to Bogotá at daybreak. I was terribly shaken. After all we had gone through, this seemed the worse. Peggy theorized that the cast had been put on too tightly. When we left the cool air of Bogotá for the hot *Llanos*, Gloria's body had swelled and the compression had caused her skin to break down. I had noticed that Gloria was fussier ever since she had the new cast. I begged Chad to go to Bogotá with us. I was really shattered by this development with my poor little baby, and I didn't feel that I could face the situation alone.

At 5:30 a.m., we awakened the children and told them that we had to go to Bogotá. They were to be good and stay with Alba. Sharon looked at me with wide, sad eyes out from under her mosquito net as we said goodbye.

The staff in Bogotá had alerted the doctor, and we went right from the airport to the hospital. A nurse held Gloria out in front of her from under her arms as the doctor used a special saw to cut off the cast. He assured me that the saw was specially made to not injure flesh, but Gloria's skin was so deteriorated that it made long gashes on her poor little legs, the scars of which she still has today. When the cast was removed, we saw that her entire body under the cast was covered with oozing sores. The nurse continued to hold her under her armpits, and I was horrified to see that even without the cast, Gloria's legs stayed in the frog-like position. She had been in a cast so long; her legs had frozen in that position. I felt the nausea and weakness of shock coming on. I was so glad for Chad's strong presence beside me.

The medical staff applied salve on the sores, then the doctor laid the back portion of the cast on a table, and the nurse laid Gloria on top of it. With elastic bandages, he secured her waist and legs to the cast. Now she was in a half of a cast. He gave me a prescription for a certain salve, and directed me to apply it several times a day.

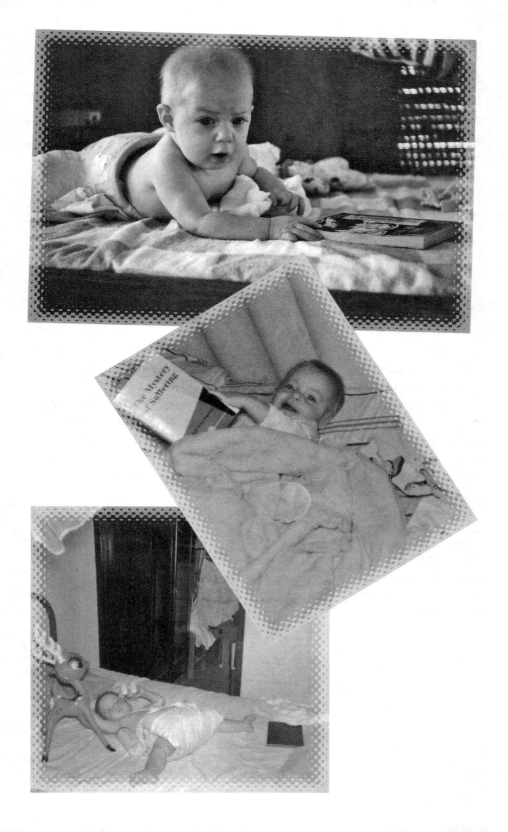

Chapter 29

Bogotá Again

Bogotá
March-April 1965

Now began a new phase of my life. It was out of the
question for me to take the baby back to Lomalinda until
this problem was solved. I would have to stay in Bogotá
indefinitely. I learned that Isabel Kerr had moved into the
cabin with the children again. After seeing the boys and
Alba chasing each other round and round the cabin with the
mop and the broom, she decided to step in. I was so grateful
to her. Sharon's little face haunted me. I kept seeing her
big, sad eyes looking out from under the mosquito net as we
said goodbye. The boys would be fine, but I really worried
about Sharon. Since I would be in Bogotá indefinitely, I was
given a room in an apartment next door to the main Wycliffe
Group House. The branch was growing rapidly, and more
space was needed, so an apartment next door had been
rented; however for the time being, Gloria and I were the
only two there in the new apartment. Chad left early in the
morning, and I was very lonely. This apartment had a large
kitchen and living room as well as three bedrooms where
missionaries could be accommodated. We were assigned
to one of the bedrooms but had the use of the kitchen and
living room as well. Three meals a day were still served in

the main Group House next door. I could sign in or out as I pleased.

This was a very long day, and towards evening I felt a respiratory illness, common to cold Bogotá, coming on. "What if I should get so sick I couldn't take care of Gloria?" I thought. I prayed for Chad and the children and tried to rest, but Gloria got fussy. At least now I could take her out of her cast, treat her sores, rub her little body and let her try to move her little frog-like legs. Everyone marveled that in spite of being in a cast for almost four months, they were still cute chubby little legs. I wrapped Gloria back into her cast again, and lay down on the double bed. It was still early, but I had nothing whatsoever to do. We had left Lomalinda so suddenly; I had not brought anything along to read or to sew. I was in a building alone. There was no one to visit with. There was neither radio nor T.V.—not even a newspaper or a magazine.

Just when I was really feeling sorry for myself, the door burst open, and in came Chad and Sharon. I couldn't have been more surprised. Sharon was delighted to see her baby sister and me again. It turned out that Sharon had developed a toothache after we left Lomalinda. When Isabel found out that Chad was returning, she sent Sharon on the plane to meet her dad in Villavicencio. He could take her to a dentist, and they could return to Lomalinda on the last flight of the day.

Sharon was so happy to see her daddy. She had always been a daddy's girl. They had lunch together and went to the dentist to get the tooth fixed. Then Chad said to her, "Shall we go the airport and get on the plane to go back to Lomalinda and the boys, or shall we get in a taxi and go see Mother and Gloria?"

"Let's go see Mommy and Gloria," was her quick response, so here they were.

Chad went to the drugstore and got me some cold remedies. We decided that he would leave Sharon with me, while he went back to Lomalinda. He would have Isabel send her clothes and first grade studies with the next group of missionaries coming to Bogotá. Soon Chad would make the trip back to the Sierra to see how Santiago was coming along on the building of our house, and to bring him back to participate in the first linguistic workshop to be held at Lomalinda in April.

Soon Sharon's belongings arrived, and at least teaching her filled up some of my time. Gloria's sores were healing nicely. She was developing a charming personality and everyone loved her. Since the cast prevented her from sitting in a high chair, I held her on my lap at mealtimes. She insisted on having a bite of everything I put in my mouth. No baby food for her, although with a little baby food grinder, I ground meat, hard-boiled eggs, etc. She never had trouble swallowing lumps as my other children had. Several times a day I let her lie on her stomach or back and kick her little legs free from the cast. Now they could assume a normal position, although they readily assumed the "frog position" when I put her back in her cast.

One day an elderly American man showed up and asked to stay for several nights at the Group House. I sat next to him at lunch one day and explained what had happened with Gloria. The next Wednesday evening after prayer meeting, he got up and spoke to the assembled missionaries. He called their attention to Gloria, and he asked that they all gather around and lay hands on Gloria and me and pray for her healing. I was very thankful for this act. Up until now much prayer had gone up for Gloria, but there had never been a united effort made like this with the "laying on of hands." Somehow this act ministered to me, and I hoped to Gloria as well.

About this time a little beggar girl started coming to the front door. She was from a very poor neighborhood but had somehow gotten into a school not far from where we were staying. In order to get home after school, she had to beg her transportation money. She was only in first or second grade but was obviously older and had been stunted by malnutrition. I was thrilled that at last I knew enough Spanish to communicate with someone like her. I gave her any leftovers that I happened to have on hand. I told her that she could come every day, and I would give her the money for her transportation. I was probably as poor as a church mouse, but this little girl was far worse off. Her transportation money was only a few centavos a day. I was still living in the apartment alone and so didn't have the problem of what the other missionaries would think. I knew that a number of them would not approve of giving anything to beggars.

Elaine Townsend was coming from the States and going to Lomalinda. She would be staying a few days in Bogotá and would occupy a bedroom in "my" apartment. I was so happy to have company, but I was kind of freaked out by having Elaine Townsend as my apartment mate. She was the wife of the famed "Uncle" Cam Townsend, the founder of Wycliffe. Although she had left their son, Billy, in our care the year before when they went to Russia, I was rather awed to spend time alone with such a famous person.

In due time she arrived with lots of luggage. The first thing she did was place family photos, a pillow here or there, and a colorful throw on the sofa in our living room. She asked me if I minded. Of course I didn't. She had transformed a rather sterile-looking public *sala* into a tasteful family living room. She explained that ever since she had married Cameron, they had had little permanency or privacy. She had learned to transform any place where she stayed for even one night into **her** home. At the time I thought it a rather nice but strange idea, but looking back I can see the value of such a habit.

While Elaine was there, my little beggar girl showed up. Elaine observed our conversation and interaction. I was rather embarrassed to have anyone witness my little charity project. To my surprise, after the girl left, Elaine complimented me for what I was doing for the girl. Later when I had the opportunity to live near Uncle Cam and Elaine at Lomalinda, I noticed that they reached out spiritually and physically to everyone who crossed their path or beat a path to their door. They showed no partiality to anyone, regardless of their race, religion, or ethnic background.

Gloria's sores were completely healed, and it was time for the new cast to be applied. I dreaded the day. I had gotten used to taking her out of the cast at least once a day for a bath and a time of kicking her little legs. She was now almost seven months old. However dutifully, I took her to the doctor and received her back again in a new wet cast. This time he made sure to leave a little room for growing or swelling in the heat. Now we were ready to return to Lomalinda. Sharon had a big pimple that had erupted on her forehead. It formed a pustule and itched terribly. The nurses helped me treat it with calamine lotion. In a few days the pustules had spread all over her body. She had come down with chicken pox.

Now our return to Lomalinda was off again. The girls and I were put in isolation in our apartment. Someone who had already had chicken pox brought our meals over. No one wanted an outbreak of a contagious disease at Lomalinda. Indian language helpers were already beginning to arrive for our first linguistic workshop. These jungle Indians came from isolated areas and could be very susceptible to white man's diseases. We had to stay in Bogotá until the contagious stage was over.

Chad passed through Bogotá on his way to the Sierra to bring back Santiago for the workshop. While he was with us, he brought home a rotisserie-roasted chicken for lunch and we ate it as a family in "our" kitchen. While we were eating, the little beggar girl came to the door. Chad invited her in and gave her a plate with some potatoes and a chicken wing. To our amazement and horror, she crunched down the chicken wing, bones and all. She seemed so hungry, we gave her the other wing. She wrapped it in a napkin and said she would take it home to her grandmother.

Sharon was over the contagion, but I thought it best to stay another week in Bogotá to see if Gloria was going to catch the disease. I didn't want to have to have another emergency flight to Bogotá if Gloria broke out with chicken pox under her cast. Sure enough, two weeks to the day from Sharon's first "pimple," Gloria started breaking out. I called the doctor, and he cut her cast in half again. Now I could take her out again, give her time to kick her legs, put calamine lotion on her pox, and wrap her back in the cast again.

While Gloria had the chicken pox, Chad returned to Bogotá with Santiago, and this time his companion was a teenaged Kogi boy named Alfonso. Alfonso looked to be about 13, but Santiago insisted that he was 15. Chad had never had chicken pox either, so he and the Kogis stayed in a room over in the main Group House. I went over to see them and to meet Alfonso. I was sure that Russell and Chaddy would be thrilled to have Alfonso as their friend. The next day Chad and the Kogis left for Lomalinda.

Gloria was getting better, and I was afraid the doctor was going to put her back in a cast again. However, one day he called me with a new idea. He wanted me to make some little straps with buckles—one for her waist, one for each thigh, and one for each ankle. He would bond these straps to her half cast with plaster, and I could take her to Lomalinda in the half cast. She would be much cooler in the half cast, and I could continue to bathe her and treat any sores that developed. Soon this was done, and the girls and I were on our way back to Lomalinda.

Chapter 30

The First Workshop

Lomalinda
April-May 1965

At Lomalinda I found another lean-to built onto one side of our little cabin. I learned it was for Santiago and Alfonso. Santiago had objected to sleeping in the dormitory with the other Indian language helpers. The jungle Indians were used to living communally and sharing everything. On the other hand, Kogis were staunch individualists. The jungle Indians had divided up a can of crackers that Chad had given Santiago to munch on, since he was not able to bring coca leaves to chew. To Santiago, these Indians were a bunch of thieves, and he had refused to live with them. He wanted to be near us, so Chad had built the lean-to. Now there would be nine of us around our little kitchen table in the middle of the cabin.

Chad and the Kogis were already involved in the linguistic workshop. I can't remember much about the workshop, but there was one important development. Alba had made friends with another girl from Bogotá named Olga. She had come to work in the dining hall during the workshop. Olga was very interested in evangelism. With the aid of

an old Indian pastor from the Paez tribe, and the backing of one of the pilots, they had started Sunday afternoon services in Spanish. During the course of the workshop, several of the Indian language helpers made professions of faith.

One interesting feature of the workshop was that Bruce Olson, author of *For This Cross I'll Kill You* (also called *Bruchko*) had come with two Motilon Indians. These Motilones were completely monolingual. Not one Motilon in the entire tribe knew any Spanish. Bruce had lived with them for several years now. Although the Motilones conversed with Bruce in their language, he had never been able to get one of them to speak into his tape recorder to help him analyze the structure of the language. On the other hand Santiago loved to record messages. One afternoon Bruce and one of the Motilones came to our cabin. Chad thought that by using Santiago as an example, he could get the Motilon to record a message in his language. Chad said, "Kogi," and gave the microphone to Santiago, who said a few words in Kogi into the microphone. Then Chad said, "Motilon," and handed the microphone to the Motilon Indian. The man took the microphone in his hand and held it to his mouth as Santiago had done. We all held our breath expectantly. "Motilon, Motilon," voiced the Indian and then handed the microphone back to Chad. That was all he would say.

A new development was that the Pepsi Cola truck found Lomalinda. Chad purchased two cases of Pepsi. We put some in the refrigerator and doled them out as special treats. When the Pepsi was gone, we had to wait until the truck came back again to exchange the cases of empties for more Pepsi Cola. At this time, each bottle of soda pop cost the equivalent of less than 10 cents U.S. To our great amusement, someone taught one of the monolingual Motilones to say in English, "There's nothing like a warm Pepsi." He soon found out that by going house to house and saying this phrase, he could get all the Pepsi Cola he wanted.

Another step of progress was that a man who had a bakery in San Martin started marketing his bread in Lomalinda. Previously we had to bake our own bread. Now we could buy very delicious bread or buns neatly packaged in plastic bags. He even sold packages of sweet bread, but since the sweet bread was made without salt, it didn't taste quite right. Later we got used to it. I still made a lot of homemade cinnamon rolls. I also kept us in chocolate cake, brownies, lemon pie, or streusel coffee cake, our family favorites.

Most of our friends were picking out lots on which to build their houses. Chad had his eye on a lot across from our cabin on Loma I. This was the main hill where the cabins and so far all the other buildings were being constructed. However, since a family had to have half of the cost of the house in hand before they could officially request a lot, we had to stand by helplessly as another family was assigned the lot.

Our Colombian neighbors continued to visit us. Many cups of cold water, as well as ice cold Pepsis were shared with the neighbors. Some came to us to ask for Aralen pills for their malaria. So far none of us had experienced malaria yet, except for Sharon's illness after Jungle Camp, but some of the other translators had suffered with full-blown classic cases. I believe we were all taking Aralen pills twice a week for prevention—all except Gloria of course.

Olga, Alba, and Don Porfirio, the Indian pastor from southwestern Colombia started visiting the nearby homes to hold evangelistic meetings. As Wycliffe members, we were strictly prohibited from evangelizing in Spanish in a formal way. (However, we had observed the Townsend's custom of personal testimony and Bible reading with all they encountered.) Since Don Porfirio was doing the preaching and Olga and Alba leading the singing, we felt comfortable taking part in these home meetings. Chad and I took turns staying home with Gloria, and the rest of the family, including the two Kogis marched off single file each evening about 6:30 p.m. to the home of a neighbor. Sometimes the two Motilon Indians tagged along too. For many nights there was no response to the invitation given by Don Porfirio, but eventually there was a real move of God, and almost all our neighbors made professions of faith. This story is told in more detail in *High Adventure in Colombia.*

Sometime while we were living in the little cabin in Lomalinda, the depression that I had known back in Bloomington, Minnesota, started returning. Although surrounded by people – when the Indians came, there were nine of us in the cabin – I was very lonely. I am definitely a "people person," and the meaningful interaction between me and the Kogis or Alba was very limited because of the language barrier. Chad was completely wrapped up with the Kogis with only a little enthusiasm left over for Russell and Chaddy. He soon was also further burdened with leadership responsibilities in the Lomalinda self-government and a growing relationship with the Colombian neighboring country men. His ability in Spanish soon far outdistanced mine.

Chaddy and Russell had developed their own lives at Lomalinda during the long months when I was in Bogotá. In addition to school, they had become very interested in hunting and fishing. Chad let them go with jungle Indians who had come for the linguistic workshop even though most of the hunting was done at night. Chaddy especially formed close relationships with the country men who had formerly been Chad's employees during the time when he was in charge of the construction at Lomalinda.

Chaddy liked to run around outside barefoot in the moonlight. Chad was sent on different trips away from Lomalinda from time to time, and I had difficulty keeping Chaddy in his bed at night on the beautiful llanos nights when the moon was full. I would have to run around outside in my nightgown looking for him. I would eventually find him and get him back in bed, but as soon as I dozed off, he was outside again. Of course, getting him up for school in the morning was another problem. One night as I looked for Chaddy, I ran into our branch director who was chasing the neighbor's burros out of his garden. I was so embarrassed that I decided to leave Chaddy to his own devices until Chad came home.

At some point during the time we lived at Lomalinda in the cabin, I felt that my relationship with the Lord was suffering. Back in the intensive spiritual atmosphere of Bethany and my ladies' prayer group in Bloomington, Minnesota, I had never anticipated that this could happen. Lack of privacy and fellowship with other like-minded women were my main problems. Our Sunday morning services led by the different missionary men were mostly geared to salvation messages. We were all from different denominational backgrounds, and no one wanted to be divisive. A message on salvation was deemed safe. Several times I inquired just who they were preaching to with these English messages and was told that our missionary children needed to hear them.

I was friends with all the women on the base, but I had not established a close, heart to heart spiritual relationship with any of them. Once or twice I went over to someone's cabin just to visit and maybe drink a cup of coffee and pray, but the lady was too busy. I was busy too, but not in the same way. The women who were what we called "support personnel," that is, people who were in Lomalinda to support the work of the translators, were assigned specific tasks. The mothers with children worked four hours a day and the other women worked eight. Their husbands might be pilots, radio men, carpenters, electricians, whatever was needed to keep the Translation base running efficiently. Some of the women were teachers, nurses, secretaries, or helped in other aspects of the base.

At this time my work was mostly taking care of Gloria and the rest of the family, and Chad took charge of the gathering of linguistic data and the well-being of the Indians. I only had to see that they were fed and that their clothing was washed. I did attend all the linguistic lectures of the workshop and accompanied Chad and the Kogis when there was a session with our linguistic consultant. Alba was a big help, but her cooking ability was limited to peeling potatoes and other vegetable preparation.

My biggest need at this time was for a little privacy. That was impossible to find in the 12 by 20 foot cabin. In the evening after Gloria went to sleep, I sometimes went out into the dark tropical night to try to pray. Here I was on the mission field, but the cares of life had crowded out the close connection with the Lord that I had known in Minnesota with the strong support of my ladies' prayer group and the church at Bethany. As I wandered aimlessly around alone in the black night, I tried to call out to the God whose presence I had once felt so intimately. This resulted in an audible sobbing sound deep in my throat. All of a sudden, I realized what I was doing. Is this what they mean by the saying, "Well, for crying out loud?" I thought.

That brought me back to my senses, and I went back into the little cabin to take up my responsibilities again.

Chapter 31

Off at Last

June, 1995

The workshop came to an end, and the Kogis returned to the Sierra. Santiago promised to get our tribal house built as soon as possible.

Chad was asked to survey the next hills on the other side of a valley that were to be known as Loma II for house sites. Just as he was thinking that a particular site would be a nice place for us to build our house, the director drove up in the group vehicle with a new couple. They decided at once to request that site. Chad was very disappointed. He poured out his heart to the Lord, "Lord, don't you have a place for us on this base?" he asked. Later that afternoon, as he was surveying the top of another hill, the Lord spoke to him. "This is the lot I have for you!" It was a fine level lot on top of a higher hill, farther from the lake but still with a view.

A few days later a letter came from Majel Meyer. Her husband's business had gone sour. She had loaded all of our cows into a truck and sold them at auction. The check had been sent to our Wycliffe account. According to my memory, in addition to our initial investment, we had gained $1,000 on the cattle venture. Now we had money to formally request the lot that the Lord had indicated to Chad.

The excitement of planning a house of our own, and packing to go to the tribe at last dispelled whatever remained of my depression.

June was here, and school summer vacation was about to start. I packed all of our tribal gear into duffle bags. We would fly to Santa Marta and then go by vehicle to Carmelo, the mission station up in the mountains that Annie Noble had told us about. Then we would travel by foot and by mule the last four hours to Santiago's house. I had questioned Santiago very carefully about what food would be available, and it seemed that there would be quite a wide variety.

Alba begged to go with us. I had mixed feelings. Avianca was giving us free tickets again for all of our family. How could we afford to buy a ticket for Alba? We had gotten out of the red, but it took careful economy to not slip back in. We told her we would make the decision after we got to Bogotá. Gloria was doing well in her cast with the little straps. Although it was only one month since we had seen her doctor, we decided to take her in for a check-up while we were in Bogotá.

We took Gloria back to her doctor the first day we arrived in Bogotá. He was surprised to see us so soon, but when we told him we were going to the Sierra Nevada de Santa Marta to live with a primitive Indian tribe, he decided to take a new set of X-rays. Usually he had us come back the next day for the results of the X-rays, but this time he sent us back to his office, and in a few minutes he followed us with the wet X-rays in his hand and a big smile on his face. The hip socket had formed!

That was the good news! The bad news was that there was a problem with the head of her femur. She would have to wear a "pillow splint" for several months to hold her legs in the same position they had been in the cast. However this would be much less of a problem than the cast. He wrote out an order for the pillow splint and directed us to a house nearby the clinic where a woman made these pillow splints to order. He estimated that it would take two weeks. To our surprise, the woman handed us a pillow splint in the exact size for Gloria. It had been made for another child who ended up not needing it. We returned to the doctor, and in a few minutes Gloria was out of the clumsy, heavy cast and into the pillow splint which was like a little play suit with a piece of hard rubber in front to hold her legs in the right position. This gave her much more freedom of movement.

The next morning I woke up with a heavy respiratory infection. That delayed us several days while Chad made a few purchases and talked with Alba on the telephone. She was still determined to go to the Sierra. Chad felt we could afford the price of a train ticket, so the day before we left Bogotá, he put Alba on a train for Santa Marta. The trip would take four days. Our family had been given complimentary round trip tickets to Santa Marta. We were off at last with our whole family to live with a Kogi family, study their language, learn their culture, and adapt as much as we could to their way of life with the goal of bringing them God's message of love and salvation in their own language. It was three years to the month since we had left our home in Bloomington, Minnesota, to embark upon this long journey of preparation that would bring us to this moment.

Would our joy and sense of victory have been dampened had we known what lay ahead?

Afterward

I hope that before you read this part, you will have already read the book. As we were getting ready to send this to press, one of my grandsons glanced at the chapter titles. "This seems like a very depressing book, Grandma," he remarked.

I was astounded! That was not the impression I hoped to give. I think the chapter titles truly depict each individual chapter, but all was certainly not depressing. There was a golden lining to most of the dark clouds. As the song goes, Above the clouds, the sun is always shining. A missionary woman who visited me during the dark days of Gloria's hospitalization quoted an oft repeated statement from the Old Testament: *And it came to pass.* And it did.

The Summer Institute of Linguistic studies were vital towards preparing us to go into a mostly monolingual tribe of people. The training of Jungle Camp was invaluable. We were some of the perhaps few people to actually put into practice all the skills we learned there, with the exception of having to build a house with only a machete and vines. Once we completed Jungle Camp, all of the challenges of primitive living were comparatively easy; we knew we could do it; we had done it before. The training we received from SIL/ Wycliffe Bible Translators was excellent for our specific missionary assignment. When Chad arrived on the scene of our first tribal location, his first thought was: This place looks like Jungle Camp gone wild.

The situation with Gloria and her physical problem is another matter. I can't say that I know why this happened, but for me, a woman who was convinced that I couldn't take care of a small baby in a primitive situation, it was an eye opener. Through the grace of God, I actually did it, and not only a normal baby, but one with a severe physical handicap. I know that God worked qualities into my life by this means. Today, Gloria is a great blessing in our lives. She is the one in the next generation whom the Kogis have selected to be their missionary.

Books in this series written by
Patricia Carlson Stendal

Minnesota Mom in the Land of the Ancient Mother

Books written by the Stendal Family

High Adventure in Colombia
   by Chad Stendal

The Guerrillas Have Taken Our Son
   by Chad & Pat Stendal

Walking In The Spirit
   by Chadwick Martin Stendal

40 Years in Colombia
Lomalinda: There and Back Again
   by Patricia & Gloria Stendal

This Gospel of the Kingdom
   by Chad Stendal

Are Millions of Christians Really Safe?
   by Chad Stendal

The Problem Christ Came to Solve
   by Chad Stendal

Rescue The Captors
   by Russell Stendal

The Beatitudes: God's Plan For Battle
   by Russell Stendal

The Tabernacle of David
   by Russell Stendal

The Elijah Who Is To Come
   by Russell Stendal

...And The Earth Shall Respond To The Wheat...
   by Russell Stendal

You can order most books from:
LIFE SENTENCE Publishing
404 N 5th Street
Abbotsford, WI 54405
715-223-3013
www.lifesentencepublishing.com

**If you would like to make a contribution
and receive a tax-deductible receipt:**

In the USA:
Chad & Pat Stendal
Pan America Mission Inc. P.O. Box 429,
Newberg, Oregon, USA 97132-0429
http://www.panamericamission.org/

All books available from:
Dwight A. Clough
1223 West Main Street #228
Sun Prairie, Wisconsin 53590 USA
Phone (608) 834-8291
books@dwightclough.com
http://www.dwightclough.com/Stendal

PARA PEDIR ALGUNO DE ESTOS LIBROS EN COLOMBIA

Colombia para Cristo:
Avenida Caracas No. 46-81 • Local
Telefax: 3461419 • Celular: 317-2219175
Correo: cpclibros@hotmail.com
http://www.fuerzadepaz.com/

Order these books from:
www.lifesentencepublishing.com
and amazon.com
(Both hardcopies and for Kindle)

Rescue the Captors,
Rescue the Captors 2
By Rusell Stendal

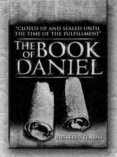

The Book of Daniel
By Rusell Stendal

The Beatitudes
By Rusell Stendal

40 Years in Colombia

A Vision is Formed
By Patricia Stendal

¿Estarán en Peligro
Millones de Cristianos?
By Chadwick Stendal

Bible in English for Kindle
Bible in Spanish for Kindle